The Young Acrobat

BY

HORATIO ALGER, Jr.

AUTHOR OF

"THE STORE BOY," "BOUND TO RISE," "BRAVE AND BOLD," "THE
CASH BOY,' "ERIE TRAIN BOY," "JULIUS THE STREET BOY,"
"PAUL THE PEDDLER," "FACING THE WORLD," ETC.

Fredonia Books
Amsterdam, The Netherlands

The Young Acrobat

by
Horatio Alger, Jr.

ISBN: 1-58963-754-2

Reprinted from the 1913 edition

Fredonia Books
Amsterdam, the Netherlands
http://www.fredoniabooks.com

BIOGRAPHY AND BIBLIOGRAPHY

HORATIO ALGER, JR., an author who lived among and for boys and himself remained a boy in heart and association till death, was born at Revere, Mass., January 13, 1834. He was the son of a clergyman; was graduated at Harvard College in 1852, and at its Divinity School in 1860; and was pastor of the Unitarian Church at Brewster, Mass., in 1862–66.

In the latter year he settled in New York and began drawing public attention to the condition and needs of street boys. He mingled with them, gained their confidence, showed a personal concern in their affairs, and stimulated them to honest and useful living. With his first story he won the hearts of all red-blooded boys everywhere, and of the seventy or more that followed over a million copies were sold during the author's lifetime.

In his later life he was in appearance a short, stout, bald-headed man, with cordial manners and whimsical views of things that amused all who met him. He died at Natick, Mass., July 18, 1899.

Mr. Alger's stories are as popular now as when first published, because they treat of real live boys who were always up and about—just like the boys found everywhere to-day. They are pure in tone and inspiring in influence, and many reforms in the juvenile life of New York may be traced to them. Among the best known are:

Strong and Steady; Strive and Succeed; Try and Trust; Bound to Rise; Risen from the Ranks; Herbert Carter's Legacy; Brave and Bold; Jack's Ward; Shifting for Himself; Wait and Hope; Paul the Peddler; Phil the Fiddler; Slow and Sure; Julius the Street Boy; Tom the Bootblack; Struggling Upward; Facing the World; The Cash Boy; Making His Way; Tony the Tramp; Joe's Luck; Do and Dare; Only an Irish Boy; Sink or Swim; A Cousin's Conspiracy; Andy Gordon; Bob Burton; Harry Vane; Hector's Inheritance; Mark Mason's Triumph; Sam's Chance; The Telegraph Boy; The Young Adventurer; The Young Outlaw; The Young Salesman, and Luke Walton.

THE YOUNG ACROBAT.

CHAPTER I.

KIT WATSON.

THERE was great excitement in Smyrna, especially among the boys. Barlow's Great American Circus in its triumphal progress from State to State was close at hand, and immense yellow posters announcing its arrival were liberally displayed on fences and barns, while smaller bills were put up in the post-office, the hotel, and the principal stores, and distributed from house to house.

It was the largest circus that had ever visited Smyrna. At least a dozen elephants marched with ponderous steps in its preliminary procession, while clowns, acrobats, giants, dwarfs, fat women, cannibals, and hairy savages from Thibet and Madagascar, were among the strange wonders which were to be seen at each performance for the small sum of fifty cents, children half-price.

For weeks the young people had been looking forward to the advent of this marvelous aggregation of curiosities, and the country papers from farther east had given glowing accounts of the great show, which was emphatically pronounced greater and more gorgeous than in any previous year. But it may be as well to reproduce, in part, the description given in the posters:

BARLOW'S GREAT NORTH AMERICAN CIRCUS.

Now in its triumphal march across the continent, will give two grand performances,

AT SMYRNA

On the afternoon and evening of May 18th.
Never in all its history has this
Unparalleled show embraced a greater variety of attractions, or included a larger number of world-famous
Acrobats, Clowns, Bareback Riders, Rope-walkers, Trapeze Artists, and Star Performers.
In addition to a colossal menagerie, comprising Elephants, Tigers, Lions, Leopards, and other wild animals in great variety.
All this and far more, including a hundred

DARING ACTS

Can be seen for the trifling sum of Fifty cents;
Children half-price.
COME ONE!   COME ALL!

Two boys paused to read this notice, pasted with illustrative pictures of elephants and circus performers on the high board fence near Stoddard's grocery store. They were Dan Clark and Christopher Watson, called Kit for short.

"Shall you go to the circus, Dan?" asked Kit.

"I would like to, but you know, Kit, I have no money to spare."

"Don't let that interfere," said Kit, kindly. "Here is half a dollar. That will take you in."

"You're a tiptop fellow, Kit. But I don't think I ought to take it. I don't know when I shall be able to return it."

"Who asked you to return it? I meant it as a gift."

"You're a true friend, Kit," said Dan, earnestly. "I don't know as I ought to take it, but I will anyhow. You know I only get my board and a dollar a week from Farmer Clifford, and that I give to my mother."

"I wish you had a better place, Dan."

"So do I; but perhaps it is as well as I can do at my age. All boys are not born to good luck as you are."

"Am I born to good luck? I don't know."

"Isn't your Uncle Stephen the richest man in Smyrna?"

"I suppose he is; but that doesn't make me rich."

"Isn't he your guardian?"

"Yes; but it doesn't follow because there is a guardian there is a fortune."

"I hope there is."

"I am going to tell you something in confidence, Dan. Uncle Stephen has lately been dropping a good many hints about the necessity of being economical, and that I may have my own way to make in the world. What do you think it means?"

"Have you been extravagant?"

"Not that I am aware of. I have been at an expensive boarding school with my cousin Ralph, and I have dressed well, and had a fair amount of spending money."

"Have you spent any more than Ralph?"

"No; not so much, for I will tell you in confidence that he has been playing pool and cards for money, of course without the knowledge of the principal. I know also that this last term, besides spending his pocket money, he ran up bills, which his father had to pay, to the amount of fifty dollars or more."

"How did your uncle like it?"

"I don't know. Ralph and his father had a private interview, but he got the money. I believe his mother took his part."

"Why don't you ask your uncle just how you stand?"

"I have thought of it. If I am to inherit a fortune I should like to know it. If I have my own way to make I want to know that also, so that I can begin to prepare for it."

"Would you feel bad if you found out that you were a poor boy—like me, for instance?"

"I suppose I should just at first, but I should try to make the best of it in the end."

"Well, I hope you won't have occasion to buckle down to hard work. When do you go back to school?"

'The next term begins next Monday."

"And it is now Wednesday. You will be able to see the circus at any rate. It is to arrive to-night."

'Suppose we go round to the lot to-morrow morning. We can see them putting up the tents."

'All right! I'll meet you at nine o'clock."

They were about to separate when another boy, of about the same age and size, came up.

"It's time for dinner, Kit," he said; "mother'll be angry if you are late"

"Very well! I'll go home with you. Good-morning, Dan."

"Good-morning, Kit. Good-morning, Ralph."

Ralph mumbled out "Morning," but did not deign to look at Dan.

"I wonder you associate with that boy, Kit," he said.

"Why?" inquired Kit, rather defiantly.

"Because he's only a farm laborer."

"Does that hurt him?"

"I don't care to associate with such a low class."

"Daniel Webster worked on a farm when he was a boy."

"Dan Clark isn't a Webster."

"We don't know what he will turn out to be."

"I don't consider him fit for me to associate with," said Ralph. "It may be different in your case."

"Why should it be different in my case?" asked Kit, suspiciously.

"Oh, no offense at all, but your circumstances and social position are likely to be different from mine."

"Are they? That's just what I would like to find out."

"My father says so, and as you are under his guardianship he ought to know."

"Yes, he ought to know, but he has never told me."

"He has told me, but I am not at liberty to say anything," said Ralph, looking mysterious.

"I think I ought to be the first to be told," said Kit, not unreasonably.

"You will be told soon. There is one thing I can tell you, however. You are not to go back to boarding school on Monday."

Kit paused in the street, and gazed at his companion in surprise.

"Are you going back?" he asked.

"Yes; I am going to keep on till I am ready for college."

"And what is to be done with me?"

Ralph shrugged his shoulders.

"I am not at liberty to tell you," he answered.

"I shall ask my uncle this very day."

"Just as you please."

Kit walked on in silence. His mind was busy with thoughts of the change in his prospects. He did not know what was coming, but he was anxious. It was likely to be a turning point in his life, and he was apprehensive that the information soon to be imparted to him would not be of an agreeable nature.

CHAPTER II.

INTRODUCES THREE CURIOSITIES.

STEPHEN WATSON, uncle of Kit and father of Ralph, was a man of middle age. It was difficult to trace any resemblance between him and his nephew. The latter had an open face, with a bright, attractive expression. Mr. Watson was dark and sallow, of spare habit, and there was a cunning look in his eyes, beneath which a Roman nose jutted out like a promontory. He looked like the incarnation of cold selfishness, and his real character did not belie his looks.

Five years before Kit Watson's father had died. He resembled Kit in appearance, and was very popular in Smyrna. His brother wound up the estate, and had since been living in luxury, but whether the property was his or his nephew's, Kit was unable to tell. He had asked the question occasionally, but his uncle showed a distaste for the subject, and gave evasive replies.

What Kit had just heard made him anxious, and he resolved to attack his uncle once more. After dinner, therefore, he began·

"Uncle Stephen, Ralph tells me I am not going back to school on Monday."

"Ralph speaks correctly," Mr. Watson replied, in a measured voice.

"But why am I not to go?"

"I will explain before the time comes."

"Can you not tell me now? I am anxious to know."

"You must curb your curiosity. You will know in good time."

Kit regarded his uncle in silence. He wished to know what had caused this remarkable change, but it seemed useless to ask any more questions.

The next morning he and Dan Clark, according to agreement, met in front of Stoddard's store.

"I had hard work to get away," said Dan. "Let us go right over to the circus grounds."

These were located about a third of a mile from the hotel, in a large twenty-acre pasture. The lot, as it was called, was a scene of activity. A band of canvas men were busily engaged in putting up the big tent. Several elephants were standing round, and the cages of animals had already been put in place inside the rising tent.

On a bench outside sat a curious group, comprising Achilles Henderson, the great Scotch giant, who was set down on the bills as eight feet three inches in height, and was really about seven feet and a half; Major Conrad, the dwarf, who was about the size of an average child of three years, and Madame Celestina Morella, the queen of fat women, who was credited on the bills with a weight of five hundred and eighty-seven pounds. She was certainly massive, but probably fell short a hundred and fifty pounds of these elephantine proportions.

Kit and Dan paused to look at this singular trio.

"I wonder how much pay they get?" said Dan, turning to Kit.

"I saw in some paper that the fat woman gets fifty dollars a week."

"That's pretty good pay for being fat, Kit."

"Would you be willing to be as fat for that money?"

"I think not," said Dan, "though it's a good deal more than I get now."

They were standing near the bench on which the three were seated. Achilles, who looked good-natured, as most big men are, addressed the boys.

"Well, boys, are you coming to see the show?"

"Yes," answered both.

"I used to like to myself when I was a boy. I didn't expect then I should ever travel with one."

"Were you very large as a boy?" asked Dan, with curiosity.

"When I was twelve years old I was six feet high, and people generally thought then that I was eighteen. I thought perhaps I shouldn't grow any more, but I kept on. When I was sixteen I was seven feet tall, and by twenty I had reached my present height."

"Are you eight feet three inches tall, Mr. Henderson?"

"Is that what the bills say?"

"Yes."

"Then it must be so," he said, with a smile.

"How long have you been traveling with the circus?"

"Five years."

"How do you like it?"

"It's a good deal easier than working on a farm, especially in Vermont, where I was born and bred."

"But they call you the Scotch giant."

"It sounds well, doesn't it? My father was born in Scotland, but my mother was a Vermont Yankee. You know Americans are more willing to pay for a foreign curiosity than for one home-born. That's why my *great* friend here" —emphasizing the word great—"calls herself Madame Celestina Morella."

The fat lady smiled.

"People think I am French or Italian," she said, "but I never was out of the United States in my life."

"Where were you born, Madame Morella?"

"In the western part of New York State. I know what you are going to ask me. Was I always fat? No, when I was sixteen I only weighed one hundred and twenty. Then I had a fit of sickness and nearly died. After recovering, I began to gain flesh, till I became a monster, as you see."

As she said this, she laughed, and her fat sides shook with merriment. Evidently she did not let her size weigh upon her mind.

"I suppose your real name isn't Celestina Morella?" said Kit.

"My real name is Betsey Hatch. That is what they called me in my girlhood, but I should hardly know who was meant if I was called so now."

"Have you been long in the show business?"

"About seven years."

"Do you like it?"

"I didn't at first, but now I've got used to moving about. Now when the spring opens I have the regular circus fever. But I have my troubles."

"What are they?" asked Kit, seeing that the fat woman liked to talk.

"Well, I find it very difficult to secure at the hotels a bed large enough and strong enough to hold me. I suppose you won't be surprised to hear that."

"Not much."

"At Akron, Ohio, where the hotel was full, I was put in a cot bed, though I protested against it. As soon as I got in, the whole thing collapsed, and I was landed on the floor."

She laughed heartily at the remembrance.

"I remember that very well," said the giant, "for I slept in the room below. Half an hour after getting into bed, I heard a fearful noise in the room above, and thought at first the hotel had been struck by lightning, and a piercing shriek that echoed through the house led me to fear that my esteemed Italian friend was a victim. But my mind was soon relieved when I learned the truth."

"I suppose, major, you never broke down a bed," said the giant, turning to the dwarf.

"No," answered the major, in a shrill, piping voice, "I never lie awake thinking of that."

"I believe you served in the Civil War, major?"

"Yes, I was in the infantry."

It was a stale joke, but all four laughed at it.

"How much do you weigh, major?" Kit ventured to ask.

"Twenty-one pounds and a half," answered the dwarf. "I have with me some of my photographs, if you would like to buy," and the little man produced half a dozen cards from his tiny pocket.

"How much are they?"

"Ten cents."

"I'll take one," said Kit, and he produced the necessary coin.

"If you go into the tent, you can see some of the performers rehearsing," suggested Achilles.

"Let us go in, Dan."

The two boys reached the portals and went into the big tent.

CHAPTER III.

KIT ASTONISHES TWO ACROBATS.

THE circus tent was nearly ready for the regular performance. Kit and Dan regarded the sawdust arena with the interest which it always inspires in boys of sixteen. Already it was invested with fascination for them. Two acrobats who performed what is called the "brothers' act" were rehearsing. They were placarded as the Vincenti brothers, though one was a French Canadian and the other an Irishman, and there was no relationship between them. At the time the boys entered, one had climbed upon the other's shoulders, and was standing erect with folded arms. This was, of course, easy, but the next act was more difficult. By a quick movement he lowered his head, and grasping the uplifted hands of the lower acrobat, raised his feet and poised himself aloft, with his feet up in the air, sustained by the muscular arms of his associate.

"That must take strength, Kit," said Dan.

"So it does."

"No one but a circus man could do it, I suppose?"

"I can do it," said Kit, quietly.

Dan regarded him with undisguised astonishment.

"You are joking," he said.

"No, I am not."

"Where did you learn to do such a thing?" asked Dan, incredulous, though he knew Kit to be a boy of truth.

" I will tell you. In the town where I attended boarding school there was a large gymnasium, under the superintendence of a man who traveled for years with a circus. He used to give lessons to the boys, but most contented themselves with a few common exercises. I suppose I should also, but there was an English boy in the school, very supple and muscular, who was proud of his strength, and ambitious to make himself a thorough gymnast. He persuaded me to take lessons in the most difficult acrobatic feats with him, as two had to work together."

"Did you pay the professor extra to instruct you?" asked Dan.

"He charged nothing. He was only too glad to teach us all he knew. It seems he was at one time connected with Barnum's circus, and prepared performers for the arena. He told us it made him think of his old circus days to teach us. At the close of last term we gave him five dollars apiece as an acknowledgment of his services. He assured us then that we were competent to perform in any circus."

"Could you really do what the Vincenti brothers are doing?"

"Yes; and more."

"I wish I could see you do it."

The boys were seated near the sawdust arena, and the last part of their conversation had been heard by the acrobats. It was taken as an illustration of boyish braggadocio, and as circus men are always ready for practical jokes, particularly at the expense of greenhorns, they resolved that there was a good chance for a little fun.

One tipped the wink to the other, and turning to Kit, said: "What's that you're saying, kid?"

"How does he know your name?" said Dan, mistaking kid, the circus name for boy, for his friend's nickname.

"He said kid, not Kit," answered our hero.

"Do you think you can do our act?" continued the acrobat.

"I think I can," replied Kit.

This elicited a broad grin from the acrobat.

"Look here, kid," he said, "do you know how long it took me to learn the business?"

"I don't know, but I should like to know."

"Three years."

"No doubt you can do a great deal more than I."

"Oh, no, certainly not!" said the acrobat, ironically.

"I see you don't believe me," said Kit.

"I'll tell you what you remind me of, kid. There was a fellow came to our circus last summer, and wanted to get an engagement as rider. He said he'd been a cowboy out in New Mexico, and had been employed to break horses. So we gave the fellow a trial. We brought out a wild mustang, and told him to show what he could do. The mustang let him get on, as was his custom, but after he was fairly on, he gave a jump and Mr. Cowboy measured his length on the sawdust."

Kit and Dan both smiled at this story.

" I am not a cowboy, and don't profess to ride bucking mustangs," he said, " though my friend Dan may."

" I'd rather be excused," put in Dan.

" I'll tell you what, kid, if you'll go through the performance you've just seen I'll give you five dollars."

The fellow expected Kit would make some hasty excuse, but he was mistaken. Our hero rose from his seat, removed his coat and vest, and bounded into the arena.

" I am ready," he said, " but I am not strong enough to be the under man. I'll do the other."

" All right! Go ahead! "

The speaker put himself in position. Kit gave a spring, and in an instant was upon his shoulders.

There was an exclamation of surprise from the second acrobat.

" Christopher! " he exclaimed. " The boy's got something in him after all."

" Now what shall I do? " asked Kit, as with folded arms he stood on the acrobat's shoulders.

" Keep your place while I walk round the arena."

Kit maintained his position while the acrobat ran round the circle, increasing his pace on purpose to dislodge his young associate. But Kit was too well used to this act to be embarrassed. He held himself erect, and never swerved for an instant.

" Pretty good, kid! " said the acrobat. " Now reverse yourself and stand on my hands with your feet in the air."

Kit made the change skillfully, and to the equal surprise of Dan and the other acrobat, both of whom applauded without stint.

" Can you do anything else? " asked Alonzo Vincenti.

" Yes."

Kit went through a variety of other feats, and then descending from his elevated perch, was about to resume his coat and vest, when the circus performer asked him, " Can you tumble? "

Kit's answer was to roll over the arena in a succession of somersaults and hand-springs.

" Well, I'm beat! " said the acrobat. " You're the smartest kid I ever met in my travels. Are you sure you're not a professional? "

" Quite sure," answered Kit, smiling.

" You never traveled with a show, then? "

Kit shook his head.

" Where on earth did you pick up all these acts? "

" I took lessons of Professor Donaldson."

2 MM

"You did! Well, that explains it. I say, kid, you ought to join a circus. You'd command a fine salary."

"Would I? How much could I get?" asked Kit, with interest.

"Ten or twelve dollars a week and all expenses paid. That's pretty good pay for a kid, isn't it?"

"It's more than I ever earned yet," answered Kit, with a smile.

"I shouldn't wonder if Mr. Barlow would give you that now. If you ever make up your mind to join a show, come round and see him."

"Thank you," said Kit.

Soon after the boys left the circus lot and went home.

"Would you really join a circus, Kit?" asked Dan.

"It isn't the life I would choose," answered Kit, seriously, "but I may have to find some way of earning a living, and that very soon."

"I thought your father left you a fortune."

"So did I; but I hear that I am to be taken from boarding school, and possibly set to work. Ralph has given me a hint of it. I shall soon know, as my uncle intimates that he has a communication to make me."

"I hope it isn't as bad as you think, Kit."

"I hope so too, but I can tell you better to-morrow. We will meet to-night at the show."

CHAPTER IV.

A SCENNE NOT DOWE ON THE BILLS.

JUST before supper Kit was asked to an interview with his uncle.

"You wish to speak to me, Uncle Stephen?" he said.

"Yes; I have decided not to postpone the explanation for which you asked yesterday."

"I shall be glad to hear it, sir."

"Ever since your father's death I have supported you, not because I was morally or legally bound to do so, but because you were my nephew."

"But didn't my father leave any property?" asked Kit in amazement.

"He was supposed to have done so."

"This house and grounds are surely worth a good deal of money!"

"So they are," answered Stephen Watson, dryly, "but unfortunately they did not belong to your father."

"This is certainly a mistake," exclaimed Kit, indignantly.

"Wait till I have finished. These stood in your father's name, but there was a mortgage of two thousand dollars held by the Smyrna Savings Bank."

"Surely the place is worth far more than two thousand dollars!"

"Curb your impatience, and you will soon understand me. The place *is* worth far more than two thousand dollars. I consider it worth ten thousand."

"Then I don't see——"

"Your father left large debts, which of course had to be paid. I was therefore obliged to sell the estate in order to realize the necessary funds."

"For how much did you sell the place?"

"For nine thousand dollars. I regarded that as a good price, considering that it was paid in cash or the equivalent."

"To whom did you sell?"

"I bought it in myself; I was not willing that the place which my brother had loved so well, should pass into the hands of strangers."

"May I ask who was my father's principal creditor?" asked Kit.

"Ahem! I was," answered Stephen Watson, in a tone of slight embarrassment.

"You!" exclaimed Kit, in fresh surprise.

"Yes; your father owed me twelve thousand dollars, borrowed at various times."

"How could he have been obliged to borrow so much?" asked Kit. "He always seemed comfortably situated. I never once heard him complain of being pressed for money."

"Very likely; he was very reticent about his affairs. I would explain, but the matter is rather a delicate one."

"I think I am entitled to know all about it, Uncle Stephen," said Kit, firmly.

"Be it so! Perhaps you are right. Let me tell you in the briefest terms, then, that in his later years your father speculated in Wall Street—not heavily, for he had not the means, but heavily for one of his property. Of course he lost. Almost everyone does, who ventures into the 'street. His first losses, instead of deterring him from further speculation, led him on to rasher ventures. It was then that he came to me for money."

"Did you urge him to give up speculating?" asked Kit.

"Yes, but my words availed little. Perhaps you will think I ought to have refused him loans, but he assured me in the strongest terms that unless he obtained money from some source he would be ruined, and I yielded. I might have been weak—it was weak, for I stood a chance of losing all, having merely his notes of hand to show for the money I lent. But it is hard to refuse a brother. I think I should do the same again."

Kit was silent. His uncle's words were warm, and indicated strong sympathy for Kit's father, but his tone was cold, and there seemed a lack of earnestness. Kit could not repress a feeling of incredulity. There was another obstacle to his accepting with full credence the tale which his uncle told him. He had always understood from his father that his uncle was a poor and struggling man. How could he have in his possession the sum of twelve thousand dollars to lend his brother? This question was certainly difficult to answer. He paused, then refraining from discussing the subject, said:

"Why have you not told me this before, Uncle Stephen?"

"Would it have made you any happier?" returned Stephen Watson.

"No."

"Till you had acquired a fair education, I thought it better to keep the unpleasant truth from you. It would only have annoyed you to feel that you owed everything to my generosity, and were in fact a child of charity."

Kit's face flushed deeply as he heard this expression from his uncle's lips.

"Do you mean that my father left absolutely nothing?" he asked.

"Yes, absolutely nothing. Well, no, not quite that. I think there was a balance of a little over a hundred dollars left after paying all debts. That is hardly worth counting."

"Yes, that is hardly worth counting," said Kit, in a dull, mechanical tone.

"Still, I determined to educate you, and give you equal advantages with my own son. I have done so up to the present moment. I wish I could continue to do so, but Ralph is getting more expensive as he grows older (and you also), and I cannot afford to keep you both at school. You will therefore stop studying, and I shall secure you some work."

"If things are as you say, I cannot complain of this," Kit said, in a dull, spiritless tone, "but it comes upon me like a thunderbolt."

"No doubt, no doubt. I knew it would be a shock, and I have postponed telling you as long as possible."

"I suppose I ought to thank you. Have you anything more to say to me now?"

"No."

"Then, sir, I will leave you. I will ask further particulars some other day."

"He takes it hard," muttered Stephen Watson, eying the retreating form of his nephew thoughtfully. "I wonder if he will suspect that there is anything wrong. Even if he does, he is only a boy, and can prove nothing."

"What makes you so glum, Kit?" asked Dan Clark when

they met at seven o'clock, as agreed, to go together to the show.

"Not much, Dan, only I have learned that I am a pauper."

"But the estate—the house and the grounds?" said Dan, bewildered.

"Belong to my uncle."

"Who says so?"

"He says so. But I don't want to say any more about it now. Let us start for the circus, and I will try to forget my pauper position, for one evening at least."

Before they reached the lot, they heard the circus band discoursing lively music. They were in a crowd, for all Smyrna, men, women, and children, were bound for the show. It was a grand gala night. In the city, where there are many amusements, the circus draws well, but in the country everybody goes.

Outside the great tent were the side-shows. In one of them Kit found his friends of the morning, the giant, the dwarf, and the fat lady, with other curiosities hereafter to be mentioned. Just inside the tent, in what might be called the ante-chamber, was the collection of animals. The elephants were accorded more freedom than the rest, but the lion, tiger, and leopard were shut up in cages. The lion seemed particularly restless. He was pacing his narrow quarters, lashing his tail, and from time to time emitting deep growls, betokening irritation and anger.

"How would you like to go into the cage?" asked Dan.

"I don't care for an interview with his majesty," responded Kit.

A stranger was standing near the cage.

"Don't go too near, boys!" he said. "That lion is particularly fierce. He nearly killed a man last season in Pennsylvania."

"How was that?"

"The man ventured too near the cage. The lion stretched out his claws, and fastened them in the man's shoulder, lacerating it fearfully before he could be released. He came near dying of blood poisoning."

Kit and Dan sheered off. The lion looked wicked enough to kill a dozen men.

At eight o'clock the performance commenced. First there was a procession of elephants and horses, the latter carrying the bareback riders and other members of the circus, with the curiosities and freaks. Then came two bareback riders, who jumped through hoops, and over banners, and performed somersaults, to the wondering delight of the boys. Then came tumblers, and in preparation for another scene a gaudily dressed clown entered the ring. Suddenly there was heard a deep baying sound, which struck terror into every heart. It was the lion, but seemed close at hand. In an instant a dark, cat-like form, rushing down the aisle, sprang into the ring.

The great Numidian lion had broken from his cage, and the life of everyone in the audience was in peril. Ladies shrieked, strong men grew pale, and all wildly looked about for some way of escape.

Striking down the clown, and standing with one foot on the prostrate form, the lion's cruel eyes wandered slowly over the vast assemblage.

Only ten feet from him, in front seats, sat Kit and Dan.

Kit rose in his seat pale and excited, but with a resolute fire in his eyes. He had thought of a way to vanquish the lion.

CHAPTER V.

HOW KIT VANQUISHED THE LION.

THE danger was imminent. Under the canvas there were at least two thousand spectators. Smyrna had less than five thousand inhabitants, but from towns around there were numerous excursion parties which helped to swell the number present. Had these people foreseen the terrible scene not down on the bills, they would have remained at home and locked the doors of their houses. But danger is seldom anticipated and peril generally finds us unprepared.

Dan Clark saw Kit about to leave his seat.

"Where are you going?" he cried.

"I am going into the arena."

"What? Are you out of your head?" asked Dan, and he took hold of Kit to detain him. But the boy tore himself from the grasp of his friend, and with blanched brow, for he knew full well the risk he ran, he sprang over the parapet, and in an instant he stood in the sawdust circle facing the angry monarch of the wilds, whose presence had struck terror into the hearts of two thousand members of a superior race.

The sudden movement of Kit created a sensation only less than the appearance of the lion.

The residents of Smyrna all knew him, but they could not understand the cause of his apparent foolhardiness.

"Come back! Come away, for your life!" exclaimed dozens of Kit's friends and acquaintances.

"Who is that boy? Is he one of the circus men?" asked strangers who were present.

"You'll be killed, Kit! Come back!" implored Dan Clark, appalled at the danger of his friend.

Kit heard, but did not heed, the various calls. He knew what he was about, and he did not mean to be killed. But there seemed the greatest danger of it. He was six feet from the angry beast, who lashed his tail with renewed wrath, when he saw his new and puny foe. Kit knew, however, that the lion's method of attack is to spring upon his victims, and that he needs a space of from twelve to fifteen feet to do it. He himself, being but six feet distant, was within the necessary space. The lion must increase the distance between them in order to accomplish its purpose.

Now it happened that Mr. Watson had in his kitchen an elderly woman, who had for years been addicted to the obnoxious habit of snuff-taking—a habit, I am glad to be able to say, which is far less prevalent now than in former days. Just before Kit had started for the circus, Ellen, who was a Scotchwoman, said: "Master Kit, if you are going near the store, will you buy me a quarter of a pound of snuff?"

"Certainly, Ellen," answered Kit, who was always obliging.

The snuff he had in his pocket at the time of the lion's appearance in the ring, and it was the thought of this unusual but formidable weapon that gave him courage. If he had merely had a pistol or revolver in his pocket, he would not have ventured, for he knew that a wound would only make the lion fiercer and more dangerous.

The lion stood stock-still for a moment. Apparently he was amazed at the daring of the boy who had rushed into his presence. His fierce eyes began to roll wickedly and he uttered one of those deep, hoarse growls, such as are wont to strike fear alike into animals and men. He glared at Kit very much as a cat surveys a puny mouse which she purposes to make her victim.

It was a few brief seconds, but to the audience, who were spellbound, and scarcely dared to breathe, it seemed as many minutes that the boy and lion stood confronting each other without moving. Indeed, Kit stood as if fascinated before the mighty beast, and a thrill passed through his frame as he realized the terrible danger into which he had impulsively rushed. But he knew full well that his peril was each instant growing greater. He could not retreat now, for the furious beast would improve the chance to spring upon him and rend him to pieces.

With curious deliberation he drew from his pocket a paper parcel, while the lion, as if stirred by curiosity, eyed him attentively. He opened it carefully, and then, without an instant's delay, he flung a handful of the snuff which it contained full in the eyes of the terrible animal.

No sooner had he done so than he gave a spring, and in a flash was over the parapet and back in his seat.

It was not a moment too soon!

The lion was blinded by the snuff, which caused him intense pain. He released the terrified clown, who lost no time in escaping from the arena, while the vanquished beast rolled around on the sawdust in his agony, sending forth meanwhile the most terrible roars.

By this time the circus management had recovered from its momentary panic. The trainer and half a dozen animal men (those whose duty it was to take care of the animals) rushed into the circle, and soon obtained the mastery of the lion, whose pain had subdued his fury, and who was now moaning piteously.

Then through the crowded tent there ran a thrill of admiration for the boy who had delivered them all from a terrible danger.

One man, an enthusiastic Western visitor, sprang to his feet, and, waving his hat, exclaimed: "Three cheers for the brave boy, who has shown more courage than all the rest of us put together! Hip, hip, hurrah!"

The call was responded to with enthusiasm. Men and even women rose in their seats, and joined in the cheering. But some of the friends of Kit amended the suggestion by crying, "Hurrah for Kit Watson!"

"Hurrah for Kit Watson!" cried the Western man. "He's the pluckiest kid I ever saw yet."

Kit had not been frightened before, but he felt undeniably nervous when he saw the eyes of two thousand people fixed upon him. He blushed and seemed disposed to screen himself from observation. But at this moment a tall, portly man advanced from the front of the tent, and came where Kit was sitting.

"My boy," he said, " do me the favor to follow me. I am Mr. Barlow."

It was indeed the proprietor of the circus. He had come in person to greet the boy who had averted such a tragedy.

Mechanically Kit followed Mr. Barlow, who led him again into the arena. Then the manager cleared his throat, and said:

"Ladies and gentlemen, I have nothing to show you here to-night that is better worth your attention than the young man whose heroic act you have just witnessed and profited by. I introduce to you the boy hero, Kit Watson!"

"Speech! speech!" exclaimed the spectators, after a liberal meed of applause.

Kit stood erect, and spoke modestly.

"I don't pretend to be a hero," he said. "I was as much frightened as anybody, but I thought of the snuff in my pocket, and I recalled to mind a story of a man who subdued a lunatic by means of it. So, on the impulse of the moment, I jumped into the ring. I am very much obliged to you for your cheers, and I wish I was as brave as you seem to think. I won't take up any more of your time, for I know you want the show to go on."

Kit retired amid a burst of applause, and resumed his seat.

The entertainment of the evening now proceeded, greatly to the satisfaction of the crowded ranks of spectators. But from time to time glances were cast toward the seat which Kit occupied.

"Kit," whispered Dan, "I am proud of you! I didn't think you had it in you."

"Don't say any more, Dan, or I shall become so vain you can't endure me. Look! there are our friends, the acrobats."

CHAPTER VI.

KIT'S POOR PROSPECTS.

THERE was one of the spectators who did not admire Kit's heroic conduct, nor join in the applause which was so liberally showered upon him. This was Ralph Watson, who sat on the opposite side of the tent, with his chum, James Schuyler, a boy who had recently come to Smyrna from the city of New York. Ralph had been very pale when the lion first made his appearance in the arena, and trembled with fear, and no one had felt greater relief when the danger was past. But, being naturally of a jealous disposition, he was very much annoyed by the sudden popularity won by Kit.

"Isn't that your cousin?" asked James Schuyler.

"Yes," answered Ralph, shortly.

"What a brave boy he is!"

Ralph shrugged his shoulders.

"I don't see much bravery about it," he said. "It isn't as if the lion was a wild one in his native forest. This one was tame."

"He didn't look very tame to me," rejoined James, who, though rather snobbish, was willing to admit the danger they had all incurred. "The people didn't think so, either. Hear them cheer your cousin."

"It will make him terribly conceited. He will actually think he's a hero."

"I wouldn't have given much for any of our lives if he hadn't jumped into the ring, and blinded the lion."

Meanwhile Kit was enjoying the performance, and thinking very little of how his action would be regarded by Ralph, for whom he had no very cordial feeling, though they had been, from the necessity of the case, close companions for many years.

On their return home, Kit and Ralph reached the gate together.

"It seems you're a great hero all at once," said Ralph, with a sneer.

Kit understood the sneer, but did not choose to notice it.

"Thank you for the compliment," he responded, quietly.

"Oh, I didn't mean to flatter you! You are puffed up enough."

"Are you sorry I jumped into the ring, Ralph?" asked Kit, good-naturedly.

"I don't believe there was any real danger."

"Then I must congratulate you upon your courage. All the rest of us were frightened, and even Mr. Barlow admitted that there was danger."

"The lion was half-tame. It isn't as if he were wild."

"He looked wild enough to me when I faced him in the ring. I confess that my knees began to tremble, and I wished myself at home."

"You'd better set up as a lion-tamer," said Ralph.

"Thank you; I think I should prefer some other business, where my life would be safer."

"You are likely to have your wish, then."

"What do you mean?" asked Kit, quickly, detecting a significance in Ralph's tone.

"I mean that father intends to have you learn a trade."

"Has he told you so?"

"Yes."

"Doesn't he propose to consult me?"

"Why should he? You are only a boy, and can't judge what is best for yourself."

"Still I am likely to be more interested than anyone else in the way I am to earn my living. What trade are *you* going to learn?"

"What trade am I going to learn?" repeated Ralph, with the assumption of insulted dignity. "None at all. I shall be a merchant or a professional man."

"And why should I not be the same?" asked Kit.

"Because you're a poor boy. Didn't my father tell you this afternoon that you had no money coming to you?"

"Yes; but that needn't prevent me from becoming a merchant, or studying a profession."

"So *you* think. You can't expect my father to pay for sending you to college, or support you while you are qualifying yourself to be a merchant."

"I don't know yet what I am entitled to expect."

"You will soon know."

"How soon?"

"To-morrow. There's a blacksmith in the next town, Aaron Bickford, who has agreed to take you as an apprentice."

"So it's all settled, is it?" Kit asked, full of indignation.

"Yes, if Mr. Bickford likes your appearance. He's coming to Smyrna on business to-morrow, and will call here. You're to live at his house."

"Indeed! I am very much obliged for the information."

"Oh, you needn't get grouty about it. I've no doubt you'll have enough to eat."

"So I am to be a blacksmith, and you a merchant or——"

"Lawyer. I think I shall decide to be a lawyer," said Ralph, complacently.

"That will make quite a difference in our social positions."

"Of course; but I will help you all I can. If you have a shop of your own, I will have my horses shod at your place."

"Does your father think I am particularly well fitted to be a blacksmith?"

"He thinks you will get along very well in the business, if you are industrious. A poor boy can't choose. He must take the best he can get."

Kit did not sleep very much that night. He was full of anger and indignation with his uncle. Why should his future be so different from his cousin's? At school he had distinguished himself more in his studies, and he did not see why he was not as well fitted to become a merchant or a lawyer as Ralph.

"They can't make me a blacksmith without my consent," was his final thought, as he closed his eyes and went to sleep.

Kit was up early the next morning. As breakfast was not ready, he strolled over to the hotel, which was only five minutes' walk from his uncle's house.

The circus tents had vanished. Late at night, after the evening performance was over, the canvas men had busied themselves in taking them down, and packing them for transportation to a town ten miles distant on the railroad, where they were to give two exhibitions the next day. The showy chariots, the lions, tigers, elephants and camels, with all the performers, were gone. But Mr. Barlow, the owner of the circus, had remained at the Smyrna Hotel all night, preferring to journey comfortably the next morning.

He was sitting on the piazza when Kit passed. Though he had never seen Kit but once, his business made him observant of faces, and he recognized him immediately.

"Aha!" he said, "this is the young hero of last evening, is it not?"

Kit smiled.

"I am the boy who jumped into the ring," he said.

"So I thought. I hope you slept well after the excitement."

A sudden thought came to Kit. Mr. Barlow looked like a kind-hearted man, and he had already shown that he was well disposed toward him.

"I slept very poorly," he said.

"Was it the thought of the danger you had been in?"

"No, sir; I learned that my uncle, without consulting me, had arranged to apprentice me to a blacksmith."

Mr. Barlow looked surprised.

"But you look like a boy of independent means," he said, puzzled.

"I have always supposed that this was the case," said Kit, "but my uncle told me yesterday, to my surprise, that I was dependent upon him, and had no expectations."

"You don't want to be a blacksmith?"

"No, sir; I consider any kind of work honorable, but that would not suit me."

"You would succeed well in my business," said the showman, "but I am very careful how I recommend it to boys. It isn't a good school for them. They are exposed to many temptations in it. But if a boy has a strong will, and good principles, he may avoid all the evils connected with it."

Kit had not thought of it before, but now the question suggested itself: "Why should I not join the circus? I would like it better than being a blacksmith."

"How much do you pay acrobats?" he asked.

"Are you an acrobat?" asked Mr. Barlow.

Kit told the story of his practicing with the Vincenti brothers.

"Good!" said Mr. Barlow. "If they indorse you, it is sufficient. If you decide to join my company, I will give you, to begin with, ten dollars a week and your expenses."

"Thank you, sir," said Kit, dazzled by the offer. "Where will you be on Saturday?"

"At Grafton on Saturday, and Milltown on Monday."

"If I decide to join you, I will do so at one or the other of those places."

Here the railroad omnibus came up, and Mr. Barlow entered it, for he was to leave by the next train.

CHAPTER VII.

AARON BICKFORD, THE BLACKSMITH.

KIT returned to breakfast in good spirits. He saw a way out of his difficulties. Though he had no false pride, he felt that a blacksmith's life would be distasteful to him. He was fond of study, and had looked forward to a college course. Now this was out of the question. It seemed that he was as poor as his friend, Dan Clark, with his own way to make in the world. When he left school, at the beginning of the vacation, he supposed that he would inherit a competence. It was certainly a great change in his prospects, but now he did not feel dispirited. He thought, upon the whole, he would enjoy traveling with the circus. His duties would be light, and the pay liberal.

Before he returned to breakfast, Ralph had come downstairs, and had a few words with his father.

"I think you are going to have trouble with Kit, father," he commenced.

"What makes you think so, and what about?" asked Mr. Watson.

"I told him last evening about your plan of apprenticing him to Mr. Bickford."

"You did wrong. I did not propose to mention the matter to him till Mr. Bickford's arrival. What did he say?"

"He turned up his nose at the idea. He thinks he ought to become a merchant or a professional man like me. He is too proud to be a blacksmith."

"Then he must put his pride in his pocket. It will be all I can do to pay the expenses of your education. I can't provide for two boys."

"When Kit is off your hands, won't you increase my allowance, father?" asked Ralph, insinuatingly.

"Suppose we postpone that matter," replied Mr. Watson, in a tone of voice that was not encouraging. "I have lost some money lately, and I can't do anything more for you just at present."

Ralph looked disappointed, but did not venture to press the subject.

"Where have you been, Kit?" he asked, as he saw his cousin entering the gate, and coming up the path to the front door.

"I have been taking a walk," answered Kit, cheerfully.

"It's a good idea to rise early."

"Why?"

"Because you will probably be required to do so in your new place."

"What new place?"

"At the blacksmith's."

Kit smiled. To Ralph's surprise he did not appear to be annoyed.

"I see you are getting reconciled to the idea. Last evening you seemed to dislike it."

"Your father has not said anything about it to me."

"He will very soon."

"Won't you come around and see me occasionally, Ralph?" asked Kit, with a curious smile.

"Yes; I may call on Saturday. I should like to see how you look."

Kit smiled again. He thought it extremely doubtful whether Ralph would see him at the blacksmith's forge.

Half an hour after breakfast, while Ralph and Kit were in the stable, the sound of wheels was heard, and a stout, broad-shouldered man, with a bronzed complexion, drove up in a farm wagon. Throwing his reins over the horse's neck, he descended from the wagon, and turned in at the gate. Mr. Watson, who had been sitting at the front window, opened the door for him.

"Glad to see you, Mr. Bickford," he said.

"Is the boy ready?" asked the blacksmith. "I can take him right over with me this morning."

"Come into the house. I will send for him."

Mr. Bickford noticed the handsome appearance of the hall, and the front room, the door of which was partly open, and said: "If the boy's been used to livin' here, he must be kind of high-strung. I can't give him no such home as this."

"Of course not, Mr. Bickford. He can't expect it. He's a poor boy, and will have to make his own way in the world. Beggars can't be choosers, you know."

A servant was sent to the stable to summon Kit. Ralph, who thought he should enjoy the scene, accompanied him.

Kit regarded the blacksmith with some curiosity.

"This is Mr. Aaron Bickford, of Oakford, Kit," began his uncle.

"I hope you are well, Mr. Bickford," said Kit, politely.

The blacksmith gazed at Kit with earnest scrutiny.

"Humph!" said he; "are you strong and muscular?"

"Pretty fair," answered Kit, with a smile.

"Kit," said his uncle, clearing his throat, "in your circumstances I have thought it desirable that you should learn a trade, and have spoken to Mr. Bickford about taking you as an apprentice."

"In what business?" asked Kit.

"I'm a blacksmith," said Mr. Bickford, taking it upon himself to reply, "and it's as good, healthy business as any you'd want to follow."

"I have no doubt of it," said Kit, quietly, "but I don't think I should like it all the same. Uncle Stephen, how does it happen that you have selected such a business for me?"

"I heard that Mr. Bickford needed an apprentice, and I have arranged matters with him to take you, and teach you his trade."

"Yes," put in Mr. Bickford, "I've agreed to give you your board and a dollar a week the first year. That's more than I got when I was 'prentice. My old master only paid me fifty cents a week."

Kit turned to his uncle.

"Do you think my education has fitted me for a blacksmith's trade?" he asked.

"It won't interfere," replied Mr. Watson, a little uneasily.
"Wouldn't it have been well to consult me in the matter?
It seems to me I am rather interested."

"Oh, I supposed you would object, as you had been looking forward to being a gentleman, but I can't afford to keep
you in idleness any longer, and so have arranged matters
with Mr. Bickford."

"Suppose I object to going with him?" said Kit, calmly.

"Then I shall overrule your objections, and compel you
to do what I think is for your good."

Kit's eye flashed with transient anger, but as he had no
idea of acceding to his uncle's order, he did not allow himself to become unduly excited. Indeed he had a plan, which
made temporary submission a matter of policy.

"What's the boy's name?" asked Aaron Bickford.

"I am generally called Kit. My right name is Christopher."

"Then, Kit, you'd better be getting your traps together,
for I can't stop long away from the shop."

"I have arranged to have you go back with Mr. Bickford
to-day," said Stephen Watson.

"That's rather short notice, isn't it?" Kit rejoined.

"The sooner the matter is arranged, the better!" answered
his uncle.

"Very well," said Kit, with unexpected submission. "I'll
go and pack up my clothes."

Mr. Watson looked relieved. He had expected to have
more trouble with his nephew.

In twenty minutes Kit reappeared with his school valise.
He had packed up a supply of shirts, socks, handkerchiefs,
and underclothing.

"I am all ready," he said.

"Then we'll be going," said the blacksmith, rising with
alacrity.

Kit took his place on the seat beside Mr. Bickford.

"Good-by, uncle!" he said; "it may be some time before
we meet again."

"What does the boy mean?" asked Stephen Watson, turning to Ralph with a puzzled look.

"I don't know. He's been acting queer all the morning."

So Kit rode away with Aaron Bickford, but he had not
the slightest intention of becoming a blacksmith. Instead
of blacksmith's forges, visions of a circus ring and acrobatic
feats were dancing before his mind.

CHAPTER VIII.

KIT'S RIDE TO OAKFORD.

OAKFORD was six miles away. The blacksmith's horse was seventeen years old, and did not make very good speed. Kit was unusually busy thinking. He had taken a decisive step; he had, in fact, made up his mind to enter upon a new life. He had not objected to going away with the blacksmith, because it gave him an excuse for packing up his clothes, and leaving the house quietly.

It may be objected that he had deceived Mr. Bickford. This was true, and the thought of it troubled him, but he hardly knew how to explain matters.

Not much conversation took place till they were within a mile of Oakford. Aaron Bickford had filled his pipe at the beginning of the journey, and he had smoked steadily ever since. At last he removed his pipe from his mouth, and put it in his pocket.

"Were you ever in Oakford?" he asked.

"Yes," answered Kit. "I know the place very well."

"How do you think you'll like livin' there?"

"I don't think I shall like it."

Mr. Bickford looked surprised.

"I'll keep you at work so stiddy you won't mind where you are," he remarked, dryly.

"Not if I know it," Kit said to himself.

He knew Mr. Bickford by reputation. He was a close-fisted, miserly man, who was not likely to be a very desirable employer, for he expected everyone who worked for him to labor as hard as himself. Moreover, he and his wife lived in a very stingy manner, and few of the luxuries of the season appeared on their table. The fact that complaints upon this score had been made by some of Kit's predecessors in his employ led Mr. Bickford to make inquiries with a view to ascertaining whether Kit was particular about his food.

"Are you partic'lar about your vittles?" he asked abruptly.

"I have been accustomed to good food," answered Kit.

"You can't expect to live as you have at your uncle's," continued the blacksmith. "Me and my wife have enough to eat, but we think it best to eat plain food. Some of my help have had stuck-up notions, and expected first-class hotel fare, but they didn't get it at my house."

"I believe you," said Kit.

Mr. Bickford eyed him sharply, not being sure but this might be a sarcastic observation, but Kit's face was straight, and betrayed nothing.

"You'll live as well as I do myself," he proceeded, after a pause. "I don't pamper my appetite by no means."

Kit was quite ready to believe this also, but did not say so.

"What time did you get up at your uncle's?" asked the blacksmith.

"We have breakfast a little before eight. I get up in time for breakfast."

"You do, hey?" ejaculated the blacksmith, scornfully. "Wa'al, I declare! You must be tuckered out gettin' up so airly."

"Oh, no, I stand it very well, Mr. Bickford," said Kit, amused.

"Do you know what time I get up?" asked Mr. Bickford, with a touch of indignation in his tone.

"I would like to know," answered Kit, meekly.

"Wa'al, I get up at five o'clock. What do you say to that, hey?"

"I think it is very early."

"I suppose you couldn't get up so early as that?"

"I might, if there was any need of it."

"I reckon there will be need of it, if you're goin' to work for me."

Kit cleared his throat. He felt that the time had come for an explanation.

"Mr. Bickford," he said, "I owe you an apology."

"What?" said Bickford, regarding his young companion in surprise.

"I have deceived you."

"I don't know what you're talkin' about."

"I don't think I did right to come with you to-day."

"I can't make out what you're talkin' about. Your uncle has engaged to let you work for me."

"But I haven't engaged to work for you, Mr. Bickford."

"Hey?" and the blacksmith eyed our hero in undisguised amazement.

"I may as well say that I don't intend to work for you."

"You don't mean to work for me?" repeated Bickford, slowly.

"Just so. I have no intention of becoming a blacksmith."

"Is the boy crazy?" ejaculated Aaron Bickford.

"No, Mr. Bickford; I have full command of my senses. You will have to look out for another apprentice."

"Then why did you agree to come with me?"

"That is what I have to apologize for. I wanted to get away from my uncle's house quietly, and I thought it the best way to pretend to agree to his plan."

Aaron Bickford was not a sweet-tempered man. He had a pretty strong will of his own, and was called, not without reason, obstinate. He began to feel angry.

3 MM

"Wa'al, boy, have you got through with what you had to say?" he asked.

"I believe so—for the present."

"Then I guess it's about time for me to say something."

"Very well, sir."

"You'll find me a tough customer to deal with, young man."

"Then perhaps it is just as well that I do not propose to work for you."

"But you are goin' to work for me!" said the blacksmith, nodding his head.

"Whether I want to or not?" interrogated Kit, placidly.

"Yes, whether you want to or not; willy-nilly, as the lawyers say."

"I think, Mr. Bickford, you will find that it takes two to make a bargain."

"So it does, and there's two that's made this bargain, your uncle and me."

Mr. Bickford was not always strictly grammatical in his language, as the reader will observe.

"I don't admit my uncle's right to make arrangements for me without my consent."

"You know more'n he does, I reckon?"

"No; but this matter concerns me more than it does him."

"Maybe you expect to live without workin'!"

"No; if it is true, as my uncle says, that I have no money, I shall have to make my living, but I prefer to choose my own way of doing it."

"You're a queer boy. Bein' a blacksmith is too much work for you; I reckon."

"At any rate it isn't the kind of work I care to undertake."

"What's all this rigamarole comin' to? Here we are 'most at my house. If you ain't goin' to work for me, what are you goin' to do?"

"I should like to pass the night at your house, Mr. Bickford. After breakfast I will pay you for your accomodations, and go——"

"Where?"

"You must excuse my telling you that. I have formed some plans, but I do not care to have my uncle know them."

"Are you going to work for anybody?" asked the blacksmith, whose curiosity was aroused.

"Yes, I have a place secured."

"Is it on a farm?"

"No."

"You're mighty mysterious, it seems to me. Now you've had your say, I've got something to tell you."

"Very well, Mr. Bickford."

"You say you're not goin' to work for me?"

"Yes. sir."

"Then I say, you *are* goin' to work for me. I've got your uncle's authority to set you to work, and I'm goin' to do it."

Kit heard this calmly.

"Suppose we postpone the discussion of the matter," he said. "Is that your house?"

Aaron Bickford's answer was to drive into the yard of a cottage. On the side opposite was a blacksmith's forge.

"That's where you're goin' to work!" he said, grimly, pointing to the forge.

CHAPTER IX.

KIT MAKES A NEW ACQUAINTANCE.

GRAFTON, where Barlow's circus was billed to appear on Saturday, was only six miles farther on. Oakford was about half-way, so that, in accompanying the blacksmith to his home, Kit had accomplished about half the necessary journey. Now that he had undeceived the blacksmith as to his intention of staying he felt at ease in his mind. It was his plan to remain overnight in the house and pursue his journey early the next day.

"Are these all the clo'es you brought with you?" asked Bickford, surveying Kit's neat and rather expensive suit with disapproval.

"Yes. Am I not well enough dressed for a blacksmith?" asked Kit, with a smile.

"You're a plaguy sight too well dressed," returned Bickford. "You want a good rough suit, for the forge is a dirty place."

"I thought I told you I did not intend to work for you, Mr. Bickford."

"That's what you said, but I don't take no stock in it. Your uncle has bound you out to me, and that settles it."

"If he has bound me out, where are the papers, Mr. Bickford?" asked Kit, keenly.

This question was a poser. The blacksmith supposed that Kit might be ignorant of the fact that papers were required, but he found himself mistaken.

"There ain't no papers, but that don't make no difference," he said. "He says you're to work for me, and I'm goin' to hold you to it."

Kit did not reply, for he saw no advantage in discussion.

"You'll get a dollar a week and your board, and you can't do better. I reckon dinner is about ready now."

Kit felt ready for the dinner, for the morning's ride had

sharpened his appetite. So, when, five minutes later, he was summoned to the table, he willingly accepted the invitation.

"This is my new 'prentice, Mrs. Bickford," said the blacksmith, by way of introduction, to a spare, red-headed woman, who was hustling about the kitchen, where the table was spread.

Mrs. Bickford eyed Kit critically.

"He's one of the kid-glove kind, by his looks," she said. "You don't expect to get much work out of him, do you?"

"I reckon I will, or know the reason why," responded Bickford, significantly.

"Set right down and I'll dish up the victuals," said Mrs. Bickford. "We don't stand on no ceremony here. What's your name, young man?"

"People call me Kit."

"Sounds like a young cat. It's rediculous to give a boy such a name. First thing you know, I'll be calling you kitty."

"I hope I don't look like a cat," said Kit, laughing.

"You ain't got no fur on your cheeks yet," said the blacksmith, laughing heartily at his own witticism. "What have you got for dinner, mother?"

"It's a sort of picked-up dinner," answered Mrs. Bickford. "There's some pork and beans warmed up, some slapjacks from breakfast, and some fried sassidges."

"Why, that's a dinner for a king," said the blacksmith, rubbing his hands.

He took his seat, and put on a plate for Kit specimens of the delicacies mentioned above. In spite of his appetite Kit partook sparingly, supplementing his meal with bread, which, being from the baker's shop, was of good quality. He congratulated himself that he was not to board permanently at Mr. Bickford's table.

When dinner was over, the blacksmith in a genial mood said to Kit: "You needn't begin to work till to-morrow. You can tramp round the village if you want to."

Kit was glad of the delay, as early the next morning he expected to bid farewell to Oakford, and thus would avoid a conflict.

He had been in Oakford before, and knew his way about. He went out of the yard and walked about in a leisurely way. It was early in June, and the country was at its best. The birds were singing, the fields were green with verdure, and Kit's spirits rose. He felt that it would be delightful to travel about the country, as he would do if he joined Barlow's circus.

He overtook a boy somewhat larger than himself, a stout, strong country boy, attired in a rough, coarse working suit. He was about to pass him, when the country boy called out, "Hallo, you!"

" Were you speaking to me? " asked Kit, turning and looking back.

" Yes. Didn't I see you riding into town with Aaron Bickford? "

" Yes."

" Are you going to work for him? "

" That is what he expects," answered Kit, diplomatically. He hesitated about confiding his plans to a stranger.

" Then I pity you."

" Why? "

" I used to work for him."

" Did you? "

" Yes, I stood it as long as I could."

" Then you didn't like it? "

" I guess not."

" What was the trouble? "

" Everything. He's a stingy old hunks, to begin with. I went to work for a dollar a week and board. If the board had been decent, it would have been something, but I'd as soon board at the poorhouse."

" I have taken dinner there," said Kit, smiling.

" Did you like it? "

" I have dined better. In fact I have seldom dined worse."

" What did the old woman give you? "

Kit enumerated the articles composing the bill of fare.

" That's better than usual," said the new acquaintance.

" I suppose the dollar a week is all right," said Kit.

" Good enough if you can get it. It's about as easy to get blood out of a stone, as money out of old Bickford. Generally I had to wait ten days after the time before I could get the money."

" How is the work? "

" Hard, and plenty of it. It's work early and work late, and if there isn't work at the forge, you've got to help the old woman, by drawing water and doing chores. You don't live in Oakford, do you? "

" No; I came from Smyrna."

" I thought not. Bickford can't get a boy to work for him here. What made you come? Couldn't you get a place at home? "

" I didn't try."

" Well, you haven't done much in coming here."

" I begin to think so," Kit responded, with a smile.

" Hasn't the circus been in your town? "

" Yes."

" I wanted to go, but I guess I'll manage to see it in Grafton. It shows there to-morrow."

" Are you going? " asked Kit, with interest.

" Yes; I shall walk. I'll start early and spend the day there."

"We may meet there."

"You don't expect to go, do you? Bickford won't let you off."

Kit smiled.

"I don't think Mr. Bickford will have much to say about it," he said.

"Are you going to hook jack?" asked his new acquaintance.

"I didn't mean to tell you, but I will. I have made up my mind not to work for Mr. Bickford at all."

"Then why did you come here?"

"Because my uncle saw fit to arrange with him."

"What are you going to do, then?"

"I am offered work with the circus."

"You are!" exclaimed the country boy, opening wide his eyes in astonishment. "What are you going to do?"

"I am going to be an acrobat."

"What's that?"

Kit explained as well as he could.

"What are they going to pay you?"

"Ten dollars a week and my expenses," answered Kit, proudly.

"Jehu!" ejaculated the other boy. "Why, that's good wages for a man. Do you think they'd hire me too?"

"If you think you can do what they require, you can ask them."

"Why can't I do it as well as you?"

"Because I have been practicing for a long time at a gymnasium. What is your name?"

"Bill Morris."

"Then, Bill, don't say a word to anyone about my plans. Suppose we go to Grafton together?"

"All right!"

Before the boys parted they made an agreement to meet at five o'clock the next morning, to set out on their walk to Grafton.

CHAPTER X.

KIT'S FIRST NIGHT AT THE BLACKSMITH'S.

AT nine o'clock the blacksmith, giving a deep yawn, said: "You'd better be getting to bed, young feller. You'll have to be up bright and airly in the morning."

Kit was already feeling sleepy, and made no objection. Though it was yet early, he had found it hard work to get through the evening, as he could find nothing to read except a weekly paper, three months old, and a copy of "Pilgrim's Progress." In truth, neither Mr. Bickford nor his wife was of a literary turn, and did not even manage to keep up with the news of the day.

"I am ready," said Kit.

"Mother, show him to his room," added the blacksmith. "To-morrow I'll give him a lesson at the forge."

"Perhaps you will," said Kit to himself, "but I think it doubtful."

Kit's room was a small back one on the second floor. The front apartment was occupied by Mr. and Mrs. Bickford, and there was one of the same size which was used as a spare chamber.

Kit's room was supplied with a cot bed, and was furnished in the plainest manner. One thing he missed. He saw no washstand.

"Where am I to wash in the morning?" he asked.

"You can wash in the tin basin in the kitchen," answered Mrs. Bickford. "There's a bar of soap down there and a roller towel, so I guess you won't have to go dirty."

Kit shuddered at the suggestion. He had seen bars of yellow soap in the grocery at home, and didn't think he should enjoy its use. Nor did he fancy using the same towel with the blacksmith and his wife. He had seen the roller, towel hanging beside the sink, and judged from its appearance that it had already been used nearly a week.

"I have been accustomed to wash in my own room," he ventured to say.

"You've been used to a great many things that you won't find here," replied Mrs. Bickford, grimly.

Kit thought it extremely likely.

"If you can't do as the rest of us do, you can get along without washing," continued the lady.

"I will try and manage," answered Kit, bearing in mind that he expected to leave the Bickford mansion forever the next morning.

"That new boy of yours is kind of uppish," remarked Mrs. Bickford, when she returned to the sitting room.

"What's the matter now?"

"He wants to wash in his own room. He's too fine a gentleman to wash in the kitchen."

"What did you tell him?"

Mrs. Bickford repeated her remark.

"Good for you, mother! We'll take down his pride a little."

"Is he goin' to work in them fine clo'es he brought with him?"

"He didn't bring any others."

"He'll spile 'em, and not have anything to wear to meetin'."

"Haven't we got a pair of overalls in the house—one that the last boy used?"

"Yes; I'll get 'em right away."

"They'll be good for him to wear."

Before Kit got into bed, the door of his chamber was unceremoniously opened, and Mrs. Bickford walked in, carrying a faded pair of overalls.

"You can put these on in the mornin'," she said. "They'll keep your clo'es clean. They may be a mite long for you, but you can turn up the legs at the bottom."

She left the room without waiting for an answer.

Kit surveyed the overalls with amusement.

"I wonder how I should look in them," he said to himself.

He drew them on over his trousers and regarded his figure as well as he could in the little seven-by-nine glass that hung on the wall.

"There is Kit, the young blacksmith!" he said, with a smile. "On the whole, I don't think it improves my appearance. I'll take them off, and leave them for the next boy."

"What did the boy say, mother?" asked Mr. Bickford, upon his wife's return.

"He just took 'em; he didn't say anything."

"I s'pose he's never worn overalls before," said the blacksmith. "What do you think he told me on the way over?"

"I don't know."

"He said he wasn't goin' to work for me at all. He didn't like the blacksmith's trade."

"Well, of all things!"

"I just told him he hadn't no choice in the matter, that me and his uncle had arranged matters, and that I should hold him right down to the contract."

"I'm afraid he'll be dainty about his vittles. He didn't eat much dinner."

"Wait till he gets to work, mother. I guess he'll have appetite enough. I mean he shall earn his board, at any rate."

"I hope we won't have no trouble with him, Aaron."

"You needn't be afraid, mother."

"Somehow, Aaron, you never did manage to keep boys very long," said Mrs. Bickford, dubiously.

"Because their folks were weak, and allowed 'em to have their own way. It'll be different with this boy."

"What makes you think so?"

"Because his uncle is anxious to get rid of him. He told me the boy, till lately, had imagined he was goin' to have property. He's supported him out of charity, dressin' him like a gentleman, sendin' him to school, and spendin' a pile of money on him. Now he thinks it about time to quit, and have the boy learn a trade. Of course the boy'll complain, and try to beg off, but it won't be no use. Stephen Watson won't make no account of what he says. He keeps a horse himself, and has promised to have him shod at my shop."

"Well, it may be for the best; I hope so."

Aaron Bickford felt a good deal of confidence in himself. He understood very well that Kit was averse to working in his shop, but he meant to make him do it.

"I'd like to see the boy I can't master," he said to himself, complacently. "Years hence, when the boy has a forge of his own, he'll thank me for perseverin' with him. There's money to be made in the business. Why, when I began I wasn't worth a hundred dollars, and I owed for my anvil. Now I own this house and shop, and I've got a tidy sum in the bank."

This was true. But it must be added that the result was largely due to pinching economy which both he and his wife had practiced.

When Mr. Bickford woke up the next morning it was half-past five o'clock.

"Strange how I came to oversleep," he said. "I guess I must have been more tuckered out than I supposed. Well, the boy's had a longer nap than I meant he should. However, it's only for one mornin'."

Mr. Bickford did not linger over his toilet. Five minutes was rather an overstatement of the time.

He went to Kit's chamber, and opening the door, went in as unceremoniously as his wife had done the night before.

A surprise awaited him.

There was no one in the bed.

"What! has the boy got up a'ready?" he asked himself, in a bewildered way. "He's better at gettin' up than I expected."

Looking about him, he discovered on a chair by the bedside the overalls, and upon them a note and a silver dollar.

"What's all that mean?" he asked himself.

Looking closer, he saw that the note was directed to him. Beginning to suspect that something was wrong, he opened it. This was what the note contained:

"MR. BICKFORD: I leave you a dollar to pay for my food and lodging. I do not care to become a blacksmith. Goodby. KIT WATSON."

"I'll have him back!" exclaimed Aaron Bickford, an angry look appearing on his face. "He ain't goin' to get the best of me."

Mr. Bickford harnessed up his horse, and started after the fugitive. But in what direction should he drive? He was not long at fault. He met a milkman, who had seen two boys starting out on the Grafton road and so informed him.

"I guess they're bound for the circus," he said.

"Like as not," returned the blacksmith.

But he had a long chase of it. It was not until he was within half a mile of the circus tents that he descried the two boys trudging along, Kit with his valise in his hand. Hearing the sound of wheels, the boys looked back, and in some dismay recognized their pursuer.

The blacksmith stood up in his wagon, and pointing his long whip at Kit, cried out: "Stop where you are, Kit Watson, or I'll give you the worst thrashing you ever had!"

CHAPTER XI.

KIT FALLS INTO THE HANDS OF THE ENEMY.

IF Aaron Bickford expected to frighten Kit by his threat, he was destined to find himself badly mistaken.

Kit was startled at first, not having anticipated that the blacksmith would get upon his track so soon. But he was a boy of spirit, and had no thought of surrender. Mr. Bickford halted his horse, and Kit faced him.

"Didn't you find my note?" he asked.

"Yes, I did."

"Then you know that I don't care to work for you."

"What's that got to do with it? Your uncle and me have settled that you shall."

"Then you'll have to unsettle it. I have a right to choose my own occupation, and I don't intend to become a blacksmith. Even if I did, I should choose someone else as my teacher."

"None of your impudence, young man! You'll have a long account to settle with me, I warn you of that."

"I had but one account to settle—for my board and lodging—and I've attended to that. Good-morning, Mr. Bickford."

Kit turned and began to continue his journey.

"Hallo! Stop, I tell you!" shouted the blacksmith.

"Have you got any more to say? If so, I'll listen."

"What more I have to say, I shall say with a horsewhip!" retorted Bickford, grimly, preparing to descend from his wagon.

"Come, William, we must run for it," said Kit. "Are you good at running?"

"Try me!" was the laconic reply.

By the time Aaron Bickford was out of his wagon, the boys had increased the distance between them by several rods.

"Oho, so that's your game, is it?" said the blacksmith. "If I don't overhaul them, my name isn't Aaron Bickford."

Kit was a good runner—quite as good as his pursuer— but he had one serious disadvantage. His valise was heavy and materially affected his speed. He had carried it several miles, and though he had shifted it from one hand to the other, both arms were now tired.

"Let me take it, Kit," said his companion, who was now on intimate terms with him.

"It'll be just as heavy for you as for me."

"Never mind! He isn't after me."

"Well, if you don't mind carrying it a little while."

The advantage of the change was soon apparent. Kit increased his speed, and William, whose arms were not tired, was not materially retarded by his burden.

"If I had no valise I would climb a tree," said Kit, while running. "I don't believe Mr. Bickford is good at climbing."

"We haven't got far to go to reach the circus tents," returned William.

But though the boys held out well, Aaron Bickford gradually gained upon them. Many years at the anvil had given him plenty of wind and endurance. Besides, he was entirely fresh, not having taken a long walk already, as the boys had done.

"You'd better give up!" he cried out, in the tone of one who was sure of victory. "It takes more than a boy like you to get the best of Aaron Bickford."

It did indeed seem as if the boys must surrender. Within a few rods Bickford would be even with them.

Kit came to a sudden determination.

"Jump over the fence!" he cried.

There was a rail fence skirting one side of the road.

No sooner said than done. Both boys clambered over the fence, and with that barrier between them faced the angry blacksmith.

"Well, I've got you!" he cried, panting.

"Have you? I'm sure I don't see it," answered Kit.

"You might as well give up fust as last."

"Suppose we discuss matters a little, Mr. Bickford," said Kit, calmly. "What right have you to pursue me?"

"What right? Your uncle's given me the charge of you."

"That is something he had no right to do."

"Why not? Ain't he your guardian?"

"No."

"Who is, then?"

"I have no guardian but myself."

"That's a likely story. I can't listen to no such foolish talk."

Aaron Bickford felt that it was time to move upon the

enemy's intrenchments, and, putting one leg on the lower rail, he proceeded to climb over the fence.

But the boys had anticipated this move, and were prepared for it. By the time the blacksmith was inside the field, the boys, who were considerably lighter and more active, had crossed to the reverse side of the fence.

"Here we are again, Mr. Bickford," said William Morris. The blacksmith frowned.

"Don't you be impudent, Bill Morris," he said. "I haven't anything to do with you, but I shan't let you sass me."

"What have I said that's out of the way?" asked William.

"Oh, you're mighty innocent, you are! You're aidin' and abettin' Kit Watson to escape from me, his lawful master."

"I have no master, Mr. Bickford," said Kit, proudly.

"Well, that's what they used to call 'em when I was a boy. Boys weren't so pert and impudent in them days."

Meanwhile the blacksmith was recrossing the fence.

Kit and William took the opportunity to run, and by the time Mr. Bickford was again on the roadside they were several rods away.

This naturally exasperated the blacksmith, who felt mortified at his failure to overtake the youngsters. A new idea occurred to him.

"You, Bill, do you want to earn a dime?" he asked.

"How?" inquired William.

"Just help me catch that boy Kit, and I'll give you ten cents."

"I don't care to earn money that way, Mr. Bickford," responded William, scornfully.

"Good for you, William!" exclaimed Kit.

"You won't earn ten cents any easier," persisted Bickford.

"I wouldn't do such a mean thing for a dollar, nor five dollars," replied William. "Kit's a friend of mine, and I'm going to stand by him."

The blacksmith was made angry by this persistent refusal. Then again he was faint and uncomfortable from having missed his breakfast, which seemed likely to be indefinitely postponed.

"I'll lick you, Bill Morris, as well as Kit, when I catch you," he said.

"Probably you will—when you catch me!" retorted William, in an aggravating tone. "Run faster, Kit."

The boys ran, but again they were impeded by the heavy valise, and slowly but surely the blacksmith was gaining upon them.

Kit, who was again carrying the burden, began to show signs of distress, and dropped behind his companion.

"I can't hold out much longer, Bill," he said, puffing laboriously.

Aaron Bickford heard these words, and they impelled him

to extra exertion. At last he caught up and grasped Kit by the collar.

"I've got ye at last!" he cried, triumphantly.

CHAPTER XII.

MR. BICKFORD'S DEFEAT.

AARON BICKFORD was a strong man. By his work at the forge he had strengthened his muscles till they were like iron. So was Kit a strong boy, but it would be absurd to represent him as a match for the sturdy blacksmith.

"I've got ye at last!" repeated Bickford, tightening his grasp on Kit's coat-collar.

"Let go my collar!" cried Kit, not struggling, for he knew that it would be useless.

"I'll let go your collar when I've got ye in the wagon," answered the blacksmith, "and not till then. You, Bill, bring along his valise. I'll take ye home in the wagon, though it would be only right if I let ye walk."

"Mr. Bickford," said Kit, "you have no right to touch me. You have no authority over me."

"I ain't, hey? Well, we'll argy that matter when we get home."

And he commenced dragging Kit in the direction of the wagon.

It certainly seemed as if Kit's plans were destined, if not for defeat, to postponement. Unconditional surrender was his only choice against the superior strength of Aaron Bickford. It was certainly very vexatious.

But help was nearer than he anticipated.

They were now within sight of the circus tents, and Kit, to his joy, descried the giant, Achilles Henderson, taking a morning walk, and already within hearing distance.

"Mr. Henderson!" he called out, eagerly.

"Who is that you're calling?" asked the blacksmith, sharply.

Achilles heard, and instantly recognized the boy who had talked with him at Smyrna.

It took but a few strides to bring him to the spot where Kit was held in captivity.

"What does this mean?" he asked.

"This man is dragging me away without authority," answered Kit.

"Who is he?" asked the giant.

"He is a blacksmith, and claims me as an apprentice, but I never agreed to work for him."

"That's a lie," said the blacksmith, "he's my runaway apprentice."

"I would believe the boy sooner than you," said Achilles, not favorably impressed by the blacksmith's bulldog look.

"It doesn't make any difference what you believe," said Bickford, rudely; and he began to pull Kit in the direction of the wagon.

"Let go that boy's collar," cried Achilles, sternly.

"I won't!" retorted the blacksmith. "I advise you to mind your own business."

Achilles Henderson, like most big men, was good-natured, but he was roused by the other's insolence. He carried war into the enemy's camp by seizing the blacksmith and shaking him till he was compelled to release his grasp.

"What do you mean by this outrage?" demanded Bickford, furiously.

"It's only a gentle hint," said Achilles, smiling; "now, my friend, I've got a piece of advice to give you. If that is your wagon back there you'd better get into it as soon as convenient—the sooner the better—and get out of my way, or I'll give you a stronger hint."

The blacksmith was too indignant to be prudent. What! Confess himself vanquished, and go home without the boy! The idea was intolerable to him.

"I'm goin' to take the boy," he said, angrily, and darting forward he essayed to seize Kit by the collar again.

"Oho! You need a stronger hint," said Achilles. With this he grasped the blacksmith about the middle, and tossed him over the fence into the adjoining field as easily as if he were a cat.

Aaron Bickford did not know what had happened to him. He lay motionless for a few seconds, and then picked himself up with some difficulty, and confronted the giant with mingled fear and anger.

"I'll have the law of ye for this," he shouted.

Achilles laughed.

"It's as you like," he said. "I've got my witnesses here," pointing to the two boys.

Mr. Bickford got over the fence, and sullenly turned in the direction of his deserted wagon.

"You'll hear from me again, all of you!" he shouted, shaking his fist.

"Don't trouble yourself to write," said the giant, jocosely. "We can worry along without a letter."

The blacksmith was too full of wrath for utterance. He kept on his way, muttering to himself, and shaking his fist at intervals.

"Now what's all this about?" asked Achilles. "What's the matter with our amiable friend?"

Kit explained.

" So you don't want to be a blacksmith? Where are you going, if I may inquire? "

" I'm going to join the circus," answered Kit.

" In what capacity—as a lion-tamer? "

" No; I shouldn't fancy that business. I am to be an acrobat."

" An acrobat! But are you qualified? " asked Achilles, somewhat surprised.

He had not heard of Kit's practice with the Vincenti brothers on the day of his first visit to the circus.

" I am pretty well qualified already," answered Kit. " I saw Mr. Barlow yesterday morning, and he promised me an engagement at ten dollars a week."

" Good! " said Achilles, heartily. " I am pleased to hear it. I took a liking to you the other day, and I'm glad you're going to join us. But do you think it wise to choose such a life? "

" You have chosen it," said Kit.

" Yes; but what could I do—a man of my size? I must earn more than a common man. My board and clothes both cost more. What do you think I paid for this suit I have on? "

" I couldn't tell, sir."

" Sixty dollars. The tailor only charges thirty dollars to a man of ordinary size, but I am so absurdly large that I have to pay double price."

" Why don't you buy your suits ready made? " asked Kit, smiling.

Achilles laughed heartily at the idea.

" Show me a place where I can get ready-made clothes to fit me," he answered, " and I will gladly accept your suggestion."

" That may be a little difficult, I admit."

" Why, you have no idea how inconvenient I find it to be so large. I can't find a bed to suit me in any hotel. If I go to the theater, I can't crowd myself into an ordinary seat. I have to have all kinds of clothing, inside and outside, made to order. My hats and shoes must also be made expressly for me."

" I suppose you get very well paid," suggested Kit.

" Seventy-five dollars a week sounds pretty large, and would be if my expenses were not so great. You wouldn't be a giant for that money, would you? "

" I am not so ambitious," replied Kit, smiling. " But there was a moment when I wished myself of your size."

" When was that? "

" When the blacksmith grasped me by the collar."

" You don't have to work very hard," said William Morris.

" My boy, it is pretty hard work to be stared at by a crowd

of people. I get tired of it often, but I see no other way of making a living."

"You would make a pretty good blacksmith."

"I couldn't earn more than a man of average strength, and that wouldn't be enough, as I have explained."

"Were your parents very tall?" asked Kit.

"My father was six feet in height, but my mother was a small woman. I don't know what put it into me to grow so big. But here we are at the lot. Will you come in?"

"When can I see Mr. Barlow?" asked Kit, anxiously.

"He is at the hotel. He won't be round till half-past nine. Have you two boys had breakfast?"

"No," answered Kit; "I'm nearly famished."

"Come round to the circus tent. You are to be one of us, and will board there. I guess we can provide for your friend, too."

Never was invitation more gladly accepted. Both Kit and William felt as if they had not broken their fast for a week.

CHAPTER XIII.

BREAKFAST IN THE CIRCUS TENT.

ACHILLES entered the circus inclosure—the "lot," as it is generally called,—and made his way to a small tent situated not far from the one devoted to the performances. An attendant was carrying in a plate of hot steak and potatoes from the cook tent near by.

"Is breakfast ready?" asked Achilles.

"Yes; any time you want it."

"Is anybody inside?"

"Only Mlle. Louise."

"Well, I want three breakfasts—for myself and my two young friends here."

"I didn't know you had sons," said Mike, the attendant, regarding Kit and William with some curiosity.

"I haven't. One of these young men is an acrobat, who will be one of us. The other is his friend. Bring along the grub as quick as possible—we are all hungry."

"All right, sir."

Running the length of the tent, which was about twenty feet by ten, was a long table surrounded by benches.

The giant took his seat and placed the boys one on each side of him. Just opposite sat a woman of twenty-five or thereabouts, who was already eating breakfast.

"Good-morning, Mlle. Louise," said the giant.

"Good-morning, Mr. Henderson," responded the lady. "Who are your young companions?"

"I don't know their names, but this one," placing his hand on Kit's shoulder, "has been engaged by Mr. Barlow as an acrobat."

"Indeed! He looks young."

"I am sixteen," volunteered Kit.

"What circus have you traveled with before this season?" asked Mlle. Louise.

"I have never traveled with any, Madam."

"But you are an acrobat?"

"I have had my practice in a gymnasium."

"How came Mr. Barlow to engage you?"

"At Smyrna I practiced a little with the Vincenti brothers."

"At Smyrna? Why, that's where the lion dashed into the arena!"

"Yes."

"Do you know the boy who had the courage to face him?"

Kit blushed.

"I am the boy," he said.

"You don't mean it!" exclaimed the lady, vivaciously. "Why, you're a hero. I must shake hands with you," and she reached across the table and gave Kit a hearty grasp of the hand.

"Is that so?" interposed Achilles. "Why, I didn't know you were the boy. I was not present at the time, and only heard of it afterwards. Mlle. Louise is right. You are a brave fellow."

"I am much obliged to you both for your favorable opinion," said Kit, modestly, "but I didn't realize my danger till afterwards."

"Oh, heavens! I can see him now—that wicked beast!" exclaimed the lady. "I was nearly scared out of my senses. As to poor Dupont, he was nearer death than I ever want to be till my time comes."

"Was Dupont the clown?" asked Kit.

"Yes. The lion held him down, with his foot upon the poor clown's back, and but for your brave act he would have torn the poor fellow to pieces. Mr. Henderson, you missed the most thrilling act of the evening."

"So I begin to think. By the way, boys, I ought to have introduced this lady. She is the famous aérial artist whom you saw the other evening in her wonderful feats upon the trapeze."

"Yes," said Mlle. Louise, complacently, "I think I have a pretty good act. I get plenty of applause; eh, Mr. Henderson?"

"That's true. I think I should leave the circus if I had to appear in your act. I never could summon up courage."

The lady laughed.

"Monsieur Achilles," she said, "I wouldn't advise you to emulate me. I don't believe you could find a rope strong enough to support you, and if you should fall, I pity the audience."

"You have convinced me. I shall give up all thoughts of it," said the giant, with mock gravity. "It would suit better our young friend here, who is an acrobat."

"Did you ever practice on a trapeze?" asked Mlle. Louise, turning to Kit.

"Yes, often," answered Kit, "but never at a great height."

"Would it frighten you to find yourself so high up in the air?"

"I don't think so; I have a cool head."

"You must practice. I will give you a few hints myself. If you are cool and courageous, as I judge, you will soon learn. By the way, what is your name?"

"Kit Watson."

"It'll be something else when you begin work."

"Do all performers have assumed names?"

"Generally. Here I am Mademoiselle Louise Lefroy, but it isn't a bit like my real name."

Before this the boys had been served with breakfast. The steak was rather tough, and the coffee not of the best quality, but Kit and William thoroughly enjoyed it, and thought it about the best breakfast they had ever eaten. Mlle. Louise continued to converse with them, and was very gracious.

"Are you too an acrobat?" she asked William.

William became so confused that he swallowed some coffee the wrong way, and came near choking.

"No, ma'am," he answered, bashfully, "but I'd like to go round with the show."

"You'll be better off at home if you've got one," said the giant. "You are not a performer; you are too small for a property man, and not strong enough for a razorback."

"What's a razorback?" asked William, in amazement.

Achilles smiled.

"It's a boy or man who helps load and unload the circus cars," he answered. "It is heavy work, and you would be thrown among a low lot of people—canvas men, and such. Our young friend here, on the other hand, will have a good sleeping berth, eat at the first table, and be well provided for generally."

William looked disappointed. He had never thought particularly about traveling with a circus till now, but his meeting with Kit had given him a circus fever.

At ten o'clock Mr. Barlow came to the grounds, and Achilles volunteered to go with Kit to speak with him about his engagement.

CHAPTER XIV.

SOME CIRCUS PEOPLE.

MR. BARLOW recognized Kit instantly.

"So you have kept your promise, my young friend," he said. "Well, have you come to join us?"

"Yes, sir, if your offer holds good."

"My offers always hold good; I never go back on my word."

Kit was glad to hear this, for he would have been placed in an embarrassing position if, like some men, Mr. Barlow had forgotten an offer made on the impulse of the moment.

"Have you any directions to give, sir?"

"You may report to my manager, Mr. Bryant. First, however, it may be well for you to see the Vincenti brothers, and arrange for a joint act."

"When do you wish me to appear, sir?"

"Whenever you are ready. You make take a week to rehearse, if necessary. Your pay will commence at once."

"Thank you, Mr. Barlow; you are very kind and considerate."

Mr. Barlow smiled, and, waving his hand, passed on.

He was very popular with all who were in his employ, and had a high reputation for kindness and strict integrity.

"I'd like to work for him," said William Morris, who had listened to the conversation between Kit and the circus proprietor.

"I should like to have you along with me," replied Kit, "but from what Mr. Henderson says there is no good opening."

It was not till eleven o'clock that Kit met his future partners, the Vincenti brothers.

"Good!" said Alonzo, in a tone of satisfaction. "We must get up a joint act. I suppose you haven't got a suit of tights?"

"No. I never expected to need one."

"I have an extra one which I think will fit you. Though I am ten years older than you, we are about the same size."

Kit had occasion to remark that circus performers are short as a rule. Many of them do not exceed five feet four inches in height, but generally they are compactly built, with well-developed muscles, and possess unusual strength and agility.

The circus suit was brought out. It proved to be an excellent fit.

William Morris eyed Kit with admiration.

"You look like a regular circus chap, Kit!" he exclaimed. "I wish I was in your shoes."

"Wait till you see whether I am a success, William," replied Kit.

"Now, if you are ready, we will have a little practice," said Alonzo Vincenti.

"May I look on?" asked William.

"Oh, yes; we don't generally admit spectators, but you are a friend of the boy."

They all entered the tent, and for an hour Kit was kept hard at work.

In the act devised by the Vincenti brothers, he stood on the shoulders of the second, who in his turn stood on the shoulders of the first. Various changes were gone through, in all of which Kit proved himself an adept, and won high compliments from his new associates.

"Can you tumble?" asked Antonio.

Kit smiled.

"I was afraid I should when I first got on your shoulders," he answered.

"That was what I meant,—something like this," and he whirled across the arena, rolling over and over on hands and feet in the manner of a cart wheel.

Kit imitated Antonio rather slowly and awkwardly at first, but rapidly showed improvement.

"You'll soon learn," said Antonio. "Now let me show you something else."

This something else was a succession of somersaults, made in the most rapid manner.

Kit tried this also, slowly at first, as before, but proving a rapid learner.

"In the course of three or four days you will be able to do it in public," said Alonzo.

"When do you advise me to make my first appearance?" asked Kit.

"To-night, in our first act."

"But shall I be ready?"

"You'll do. We may as well make a beginning."

"I wish I could see you, Kit," said William.

"Can't you?"

"I was going to the afternoon performance. It would make me too late home if I stayed in the evening."

"Won't there be some people over from Oakford that you can ride back with?"

"I didn't think of that. Yes, John Woods told me that his father was coming, and would bring him along. I could ride home with them."

"Good! then you'd better stay."

"Perhaps I'd better go over and buy a ticket."

But to William's satisfaction he was given free admission as a friend of Kit. Not only that, but he was invited to take dinner and supper at the circus table. In fact, he was treated with distinguished consideration.

"Kit," he said, "I was in luck to meet you."

"And it was lucky for me that I met you. I shouldn't like to have met Aaron Bickford singlehanded."

"I wish old Bickford would come to the circus to-night. Wouldn't he be surprised to see you performing in tights?"

"I think it would rather take him by surprise," said Kit, smiling.

Kit and William occupied seats at the afternoon performance as spectators, it having been arranged that Kit's *début* should be made in the evening. Our hero regarded the different acts with unusual interest, and his heart beat a little quicker when he heard the applause elicited by the performances of the Vincenti brothers, for he had already begun to consider himself one of them.

When the performance was over, and the audience was dispersing, Kit felt a hand laid upon his shoulder.

He turned, and his glance rested upon a man of about forty, with a grave, serious expression. He was puzzled, for it was not a face that he remembered to have ever seen before.

"You don't know me?" said the stranger.

"No, sir."

"And yet you have done me a very great service."

"I didn't know it, sir."

"The greatest service that any one person can do to another—you have saved my life."

Then a light dawned upon Kit's mind, and he remembered what Achilles Henderson had said to him in the morning.

"Is your name Dupont?" he asked.

"Yes; I am Joe Dupont, the clown, whom you saved from a horrible death. I tell you, when Nero stood there in the ring with his paw on my breast I gave myself up for lost. I expected to be torn to pieces. It was an awful moment!" and the clown shuddered at the picture which his imagination conjured up. "Yes, sir; I wouldn't see such another moment for all the money Barlow is worth. I wonder my hair didn't turn white."

"Excuse me, Mr. Dupont, but I find it hard to think you are Joe Dupont, the clown," said Kit.

"Why?"

"Because you look so grave and sedate."

Joe Dupont smiled.

"I only make a fool of myself in the ring," he said. "Outside you might take me for a merchant or minister. Indeed, I am a minister's son."

"You a minister's son!" ejaculated Kit.

"Yes; you wouldn't think it, would you? I was rather a wild lad, as minister's sons often are. My poor father tried hard to give me an education, but my mind wasn't on books or school exercises, and at sixteen I cut and run."

"Did you join a circus then?"

"Not at once. I tried hard to earn my living in different ways. Finally I struck a circus, and got an engagement as a razorback. When I got older I began to notice and imitate the clowns, and finally I made up my mind to become one myself."

"Do you like the business?"

"I have to like it. No; I am disgusted with myself often and often. You can judge from one thing. I have a little daughter, Katy, now eight years of age. She has never seen me in the ring and never will. I could never hold up my head in her presence if she had once seen me playing the fool before an audience."

All this surprised Kit. He had been disposed to think that what clowns were before the public they were in private life also. Now he saw his mistake.

"You contribute to the public amusement, Mr. Dupont," said Kit.

"True; but what sort of a life record is it? Suppose in after years Katy is asked, 'Who was your father?' and is obliged to answer, 'Joe Dupont, the clown.' But I ought not to grumble. But for you I should have died a terrible death, and Katy would be fatherless, so I have much to be thankful for after all."

Kit listened to the clown not without surprise. He could hardly realize that this was the comical man whose grotesque actions and sayings had convulsed the spectators only an hour before. When he came to think of it, he felt that he would rather be an acrobat than a clown.

CHAPTER XV.

MR. BICKFORD GOES TO THE CIRCUS.

WHEN Aaron Bickford, balked of his prey, was compelled to get into his wagon and start for home, he felt uncommonly cross. To begin with, he was half famished, having harnessed up and set out on what turned out to be a wild-goose chase without breaking his fast. Yet he could have borne this with comparative equanimity if he had effected the purpose which he had in view—the capture of his expected apprentice.

But he had been signally defeated. Indeed he had been humiliated in presence of Kit and William Morris, by being unceremoniously picked up and tossed over the fence. As William was an Oakford boy, he foresaw that his discomfiture would soon be known to all his fellow townsmen, and that public ridicule would be his portion. There seemed no way to avoid this, unless by begging William to keep silent, and this he could not bring himself to do, even if the request was likely to be granted.

"Where's the boy?" asked his wife, as, after unharnessing his horse, he went into the house.

"I don't know where he is," answered Bickford, in a surly tone.

"Didn't you find him?"

"Yes, I found him."

"Wouldn't he come back?"

"He didn't."

"I'd have made him if I were you."

"Perhaps you would, and then perhaps you wouldn't. Perhaps you couldn't."

"You don't mean to say, Aaron Bickford, that you let a whippersnapper like that defy you?"

"What could I do against a man eight feet high?"

"Goodness, Mr. Bickford, have you been drinking?" ejaculated his wife.

"No, I haven't been drinking."

"Do you mean to tell me that boy is eight feet high?"

"No, I don't mean to tell you the boy is eight feet high. But I won't answer any more foolish questions till you give me something to eat. I am fairly faint with hunger."

"Sit down, then, and I hope after you've gratified your appetite you'll be a little less mysterious."

Mrs. Bickford was privately of opinion that her husband had stopped at some drinking place—otherwise why should he prate of men eight feet tall?

Aaron Bickford ate almost ravenously, though the food set before him was not calculated to gratify the taste of an epicure. But all things are acceptable to an empty stomach.

When he seemed to be satisfied, his wife began anew.

"Who is it that is eight feet high?" she asked.

"The giant at the circus."

"What did you have to do with him?"

"Not much, but he had something to do with me," answered Bickford, grimly.

"How is that?"

"I overhauled the boy, and was dragging him back to the wagon, when this fellow hove in sight. It seems he knew the young rascal, and took his part. He seized me as easily as you would take up a cat, and flung me over the fence."

"I wish I'd been there!" exclaimed Mrs. Bickford, angrily.

"What could you have done? You would have been flung over too," said her husband, contemptuously.

"I would have got a good grip of his hair, and I guess that would have made him let go."

"You'd have to stand on a ladder, then."

"So the boy got away?"

"Of course he did."

"And where did he go?"

"I expect he went to the circus along with William Morris."

"Was that boy with him?"

"Yes."

"They were pretty well matched. What can they do at the circus?"

"I don't know. Perhaps their long-legged friend will give them a ticket to the show."

"Aaron, suppose we go to the circus?"

"What for?"

"You may get hold of the boy, and bring him back. The giant won't be with him all the time."

"I'd like to get the boy back," said Bickford, in a wavering tone. "I'd give him a lesson."

"And so would I. I guess between us we could subdue him. But of course he must be got back first."

"I'll think of it, Sarah."

Later in the day Mr. Bickford told his wife he would go to the circus, but he tried to evade taking her in order to save the expense of another ticket. To this, however, she would not agree. The upshot was that after supper the old horse was harnessed up, and the amiable pair, bent on vengeance, started for Grafton.

CHAPTER XVI.

MR. BICKFORD AT THE CIRCUS.

Mr. Bickford's chief object in going to the circus was to regain possession of Kit, his runaway apprentice, as he chose to consider him. But, besides this, he really had a curiosity to see the show, and thought this would afford him a good excuse for doing so. The same remark will apply to Mrs. Bickford, whose curiosity had been excited the year previous by seeing a circus procession. The blacksmith and his wife were not prejudiced against amusements, like many others, but were too frugal to attend them. Now that they could combine business with pleasure, they threw to the winds all hesitation.

"Do you think you'll get the boy, father?" asked Mrs. Bickford, as they jolted over the road to Grafton.

"I'll make a try for it, Sarah. He's a good strong boy, and he'll make a capital blacksmith. Did you notice his broad shoulders?"

"He looks like he'd have a hearty appetite," said the careful spouse.

"We won't pamper him, Sarah," replied Bickford, smiling grimly. "He won't get no such victuals as he did at home. Plain food and plenty of it, that's the way to bring up boys."

"Perhaps he won't be at the circus," suggested Mrs. Bickford.

"I'd be surprised if he wasn't. Boys have a natural hankering for the circus. I had when I was a boy."

"Did you ever go, Aaron?"

"No; I didn't have the money."

"Do you know how much they charge?"

"Fifty cents, I believe."

"It's an awful sight of money to pay for amusement. If it lasts two hours, that makes twenty-five cents an hour."

"So it does, Sarah. That's as much as I can earn by hard work in that time."

"I don't know as it's right to fling away so much money."

"I wouldn't do it if it wasn't for gettin' the boy back. He'll be worth a good deal to me if I do. He's a good deal stronger than Bill Morris."

"Of course that makes a difference. I don't care so much for the circus, though I should like to see the man stand up on a horse and jump through hoops. I wonder if the horse jumps through too."

"I don't know, but we'll soon know all that is to be known. The boy won't expect to see us, I reckon," concluded the blacksmith, with a chuckle.

At length they reached the circus grounds. All was bustle and excitement in the neighborhood of the lot.

"I declare, Aaron, it looks like Fourth of July," said Mrs. Bickford.

"So it does. It beats all—what a crowd there is!"

They bought tickets and entered the inclosure.

In a small tent near the entrance were the curiosities. They were about to walk in when a young man curtly asked for tickets.

"We bought tickets at the gate. Here they are."

"All right; but you need separate tickets here."

"I declare that's a swindle," said Mrs. Bickford. "I thought we could see the whole show on these."

"We only charge ten cents extra for this."

"It's a shame. Shall we go in, Aaron?"

"I guess we will. I want to see that 'ere fat woman."

"I'd like to see the dwarf and the woman with hair five feet long. A circus is dreadful expensive, but bein' as we're here we might as well see the whole thing."

Twenty cents was paid at the door, and the economical pair, grown suddenly so extravagant, walked in.

The first object on which the blacksmith's eyes rested kindled him with indignation, and recalled mortifying memories. It was Achilles Henderson, the giant, who on his side recognized Aaron Bickford.

"Good-evening, my friend," he said, with a smile. "I believe we have met before."

"Do you know him?" asked Mrs. Bickford, in surprise.

Aaron's brow contracted as he answered:

"It's the ruffian that threw me over the fence this morning."

"I see you remember me," said Achilles, good-naturedly

"I ought to remember you," retorted the blacksmith.

"Come, don't bear malice. It was only a little joke."

"I don't like such jokes."

"Well, well; I'll give you satisfaction. I'll let you throw me over the fence any time you want to, and I won't make a particle of resistance."

Somehow this proposal did not strike the blacksmith as satisfactory. He asked abruptly: "Where's the boy?"

"There were two boys."

"I mean the stout, broad-shouldered boy."

"I don't know just where he is at present."

"Do you know why I've come here this evening?"

"To see the show, I expect."

"I've come to get that boy. I've no doubt he's somewhere about here."

"Oho!" thought the giant; "I must put my young friend on his guard."

"If you'll help me I'll do as much for you some time."

"So you are going to carry him back with you?" went on Achilles, desirous of learning the extent of Kit's danger.

"Yes, I am."

"You say he is your apprentice?"

"Of course he is."

"And you've got the papers to show for it?"

"I don't need no papers. I've got his uncle's consent."

"I think, my friend, you're not familiar with the law," thought Achilles. "Kit won't go with you to-night."

But it was nearly time for the performance. Mr. and Mrs. Bickford left the smaller tent, and entering the big one took their seats. They watched the performance with great wonder and enjoyment till the entrance of Kit and the Vincenti brothers. They did not immediately discover him, but when he stood on the shoulders of Alonzo Vincenti, who, in turn, stood on the shoulders of Antonio, and the three-storied acrobat walked round the ring, Mrs. Bickford recognized Kit, and, pointing with her parasol to the young acrobat, as she half raised herself from her seat, she exclaimed in a shrill voice: "Look, Aaron, there's your boy, all rigged out in circus clothes!"

"Well, that beats all!" ejaculated the blacksmith, gazing with wide-open mouth at Kit.

Just then, Kit, reversing his attitude, raised his feet in the air and was borne round the ring, amid the plaudits of the spectators.

"How do you think he does it?" asked Mrs. Bickford, in astonishment.

"I give it up," said the blacksmith.

"He's a smart critter. Do you think they pay him?"

"I reckon he gets two or three dollars a week, but he hain't no business to hire out to the circus folks. He's going back with us to-night, and I'll turn him out a blacksmith in two years."

When Kit had finished his act, he went to the dressing room and changed his clothes.

"I wonder whether the old fellow is after me!" he thought. "What could have put it into his head that I was here?"

As he emerged from the dressing room he met Mr. Barlow, the proprietor of the circus, who advanced toward him, and shook his hand cordially.

"Bravo, my young friend!" he said. "You did yourself great credit. Are you sure you have never performed in a circus before?"

"Quite sure, sir."

"You went through your act like an old professional. You did as well as either of the other two."

"Thank you, sir. I am glad you are satisfied."

"I ought to be. I regard you as a decided acquisition to my show. Keep on doing your best, and I can assure you that your efforts will be appreciated. How much did I agree to pay you?"

"Ten dollars a week, sir."

"That isn't enough. I raise your salary at once to twenty-five."

Kit was dazzled by his good fortune. What! Twenty-five dollars a week and traveling expenses for a boy of sixteen! It seemed marvelous.

"I am afraid I am dreaming, Mr. Barlow," he said. "I can't believe that I am really to receive so handsome a salary."

"You will realize it to-night when you collect your first week's pay."

"But this won't be a full week, sir."

"Never mind! You shall receive full pay. Do you think I forget your heroic act at Smyrna?"

"Thank you, sir. I hope nothing will prevent my continuing in your employ."

"What should prevent?" asked Mr. Barlow, quickly. "Have you had an offer from another show?"

"No, sir; I am not well known enough for that; but I saw a man in the audience who would probably like to get me away."

"Who is it?"

"A blacksmith from Oakford."

"I don't understand. What have you to do with a blacksmith?"

Kit explained briefly.

"When do you think he will try to recover possession of you?" asked the circus proprietor.

"Just after the show is over."

"Has he any papers?"

"Not one."

"Then he has no claim on you. If he makes any trouble, let me know."

"I will, Mr. Barlow."

CHAPTER XVII.

KIT'S STRATAGEM.

KIT, when dressed, sought the part of the house where he knew that William Morris was seated.

"How did I do, Will?" he asked.

"Splendidly!" answered the boy, enthusiastically. "I felt proud of you."

"I think I have a right to be satisfied myself. I have had my pay raised."

"You don't mean to say you are to get more than ten dollars?" said his friend, opening his eyes in amazement.

"I am raised to twenty-five."

"You don't mean to say you are to get twenty-five dollars a week, Kit?"

"Yes, I do."

"And your board?"

"And my board and traveling expenses," added Kit, with a smile.

"I wish I were in your shoes, Kit," said William. "Think of me with only one dollar a week."

"Would you be willing to go through my acts for the money I am going to receive?"

William shook his head.

"I couldn't do it, Kit," he replied. "It always makes me dizzy when I have my head down. I don't believe I could ever do anything in a circus."

"Well, William, I won't forget you. If I save money, as

I am sure to do, I'll see if I can't do something for you by and by. By the way, did you see Mr. and Mrs. Bickford?"

"No; you don't mean to say they are here?"

"Look over there!"

William followed the direction of Kit's finger, and he easily discovered the blacksmith and his wife.

"By gracious! You're right!" he said. "It's the first money I've known old Bickford to pay for any amusement for years."

"They came after me, William."

"You won't go back with them?"

"Not much. I don't care to give up twenty-five dollars a week for the privilege of learning the trade of a blacksmith."

"Suppose they try to carry you off?"

"That gives me an idea. With your help I'll try to play a trick on them. It'll be capital fun."

"Go ahead and tell me what it is, Kit. I'm with you!"

"My plan is that you should ride home with Mr. Bickford," said Kit.

"I don't understand," said William, looking puzzled.

"I'll tell you my idea. Bickford has come here with the intention of taking me back with him to Oakford."

"But you don't mean to go?"

"Of course not, but when the show is over I shall put myself in his way, and after a little objection agree to go. I will ask for five minutes to get ready. In that time I will charge hats with you, and as it is dark you can easily pass yourself off for me."

"Capital!" exclaimed William, laughing. "Won't the old man look foolish when he finds out who is with him?"

"Don't let him know till you arrive, or he would force you to leave the carriage, and walk home alone, and a six-mile walk is no joke."

"All right, Kit! I understand, and I think I can carry out your idea. I haven't much love for the old man or his wife either, and I am glad of a chance to get even with them."

The performance continued till ten o'clock. The blacksmith and his wife enjoyed it beyond their anticipations. Amusements of any kind were new to them, and their pleasure was like that of children.

"I begin to think, Sarah, we shall get our money's worth," said Aaron, cautiously, as the entertainment neared its end; "this is a great show."

"So it is, Aaron. I don't begrudge the money myself, though fifty cents is a pretty high price to pay. Then, besides, you'll have a chance to carry the boy home."

"That's so, Sarah. Just as soon as the show is over, foller me, and we'll try to find him."

At length the last act was ended, and the crowd of spectators began pouring from the tent.

Mr. Bickford hurriedly emerged from the audience, and began to look around for Kit. He had but little trouble in finding him, for the boy purposely put himself in his way. Aaron Bickford strode up to him.

"Well, I've caught you at last!" he said, putting his hand on the boy's shoulder.

"What do you want of me, Mr. Bickford?" said Kit.

"What do I want of you? Well, I want you to go home with me, of course."

"Won't you let me stay with the circus a week?" asked Kit, in a subdued tone.

"No, I won't. I've got the wagon here, and I'm goin' to take you back with me to-night."

"If you really think my uncle wishes it, perhaps I had better go," said Kit, in what appeared to be a wavering tone.

Mr. Bickford was quite elated. He feared he should have trouble in persuading Kit to accompany him. He would not have been surprised if the boy had disappeared and given him trouble to find him, and his unexpected submissiveness was an agreeable surprise.

"Well, boy, it's time to be goin'. Oakford's six miles off, and we won't get home before midnight unless we start right off."

"I'll go and get my things, Mr. Bickford. Where is your horse and wagon?"

"Out by the entrance yonder. It's hitched to a tree."

"All right! You go and unhitch the horse, and I'll be right along."

"But suppose you give me the slip? You'd better go along now."

"I'll bring him with me, Mr. Bickford," said the giant. "I'm sorry he isn't going to stay with us, and I'll see him off."

Achilles Henderson spoke in so straightforward a manner that Mr. Bickford was deceived.

"Very well," he said. "I'll go along with Mrs. Bickford. Don't keep me waitin', for it's gettin' late."

The blacksmith and his wife took up their march to the place where their team had been hitched. They found it safe, and untied the horse.

"We're goin' to have a dark ride home, mother," he said.

"Yes, Aaron, but you've done a good evening's work."

"That's so, Sarah. I expected I'd have more trouble with the boy."

"There's nothing like being firm, Aaron. When he saw you were in earnest, he gave up."

"I mean to keep a tight rein on him, Sarah. He's a boy that likes to have his own way, if I ain't greatly mistaken. We must break his will."

The horse was unhitched, and still Kit had not arrived. Mr. Bickford began to fear that he had been tricked after all, when two figures, contrasting strongly with each other, appeared. One was the giant, in his ample height, and the other was a boy.

"There they are, Aaron!" said Mrs. Bickford, who was the first to descry the oddly assorted pair.

"Where is the boy to sit?" asked Achilles.

"In the back seat. Mother and I will sit in front."

"All right! There you are!" said Mr. Henderson, lifting the boy in his arms, as easily as if he were a kitten, and putting him on the rear seat.

"Good-by, Kit!" he said. "I'm sorry you're going to leave us. Perhaps Mr. Bickford will let you off if we show anywhere near here."

"The boy will be at work, and can't be let off," said the blacksmith, stiffly. "But it is time we were off."

"Good-by, then, Kit!"

"Good-by!" said the supposed Kit, in a low tone, for he feared that the difference in his voice would be recognized. But Mr. Bickford had no suspicions. He was anxious to get started, for he and his wife were always in bed by this time ordinarily.

So the team started, and Achilles Henderson, suppressing a laugh, strode away to the circus cars, which were already being prepared for a midnight journey to the next place. It may be explained here that the circus of to-day generally owns its own cars, which are used for the conveyance of all connected with it, their luggage, the tents, the animals, and all the paraphernalia of the show. As soon as the show is ended, the canvas men set to work to take down and fold up the tents. All the freight is conveyed to the cars, and the razorbacks, already referred to, set about loading them. The performers, ticketmen, and candy butchers seek their berths in the sleeping cars and are often in the land of dreams before the train starts.

While Mr. Bickford was driving in the darkness to Oakford with the supposed Kit on the back seat, the real Kit was in his berth in the circus cars, preparing for a refreshing night's rest.

CHAPTER XVIII.

MR. BICKFORD'S MORTIFYING DISCOVERY.

MR. BICKFORD was in excellent spirits. He had enjoyed the evening, and although he had been compelled to disburse a dollar for two circus tickets, a sum which to him seemed large, he was disposed to acknowledge that he had received his money's worth. Besides, and this seemed to him the greatest triumph of all, he had recovered his runaway apprentice, or thought he had. He inwardly resolved that Kit should smart for his past insubordination, though he had not yet decided in what way he would get even with him. The unexpected submissiveness shown by Kit elated him, and confirmed him in the idea he had long entertained that he could manage boys a good deal better than the average of men.

"Talk about hard cases," he said one day to his wife. "I'd like to see the boy that can get the start of Aaron Bickford. He'll have to get up unusually airly in the mornin'."

Mr. Bickford felt a little like crowing over his captive, and turned his head partly round to survey the boy on the back seat. Fortunately for William the darkness was so great that there was small chance of his detecting the imposture.

"I reckon you didn't expect to be ridin' back to Oakford along of me this evenin'," he observed.

"No, sir," muttered William, in a voice scarcely audible.

"Ho, ho, you feel kind of grouty, eh?" said the blacksmith. "Well, I ain't much surprised. You thought you could have your own way with Aaron Bickford, but you're beginnin' to see your mistake, I reckon?"

"Yes, sir," replied the supposed Kit, in a meek voice.

"Ho, ho! That's the way boys ginerally come out when they try to buck agin' their elders. Not but you might have succeeded with some men, but you didn't know the man you had to deal with this time."

There was a sort of gurgle, for William was trying hard not to laugh, as he was picturing to himself the rage and mortification of Mr. Bickford when he discovered the deceit that had been practiced upon him. But the blacksmith misunderstood the sound, and thought Kit was sobbing.

"You needn't take on!" he said, magnanimously. "It ain't so bad as it might be. You'll be a good deal better off learnin' a good trade than trampin' round the country with the circus. I hope this'll be a lesson to you. You'd better not try to run away agin, for it won't be no use. You won't always have that long-legged giant to help you. If I'd done right, I should have had him took up for 'sault and battery. He needn't think because he's eight feet high, more or less, that he can defy the laws of the land. I reckon he got a little skeered of what he done, or he wouldn't have acted so different this evenin'."

William did not reply to this. He was rather in hopes Mr. Bickford would stop addressing him, for he did not like to run the risk of answering, as it might open the eyes of the blacksmith to the fact that he had the wrong boy in the wagon.

The distance to Oakford steadily diminished, though Mr. Bickford's horse was a slow one. At length it had dwindled to half a mile.

"Now I don't care if he does find out who I am," thought William. "It ain't but a little way home now, and I shouldn't mind walking." Still his own house was rather beyond Mr. Bickford's, and it was just as well to ride the whole way, if he could escape detection so long.

"Where did you learn them circus performances, Christopher?" suddenly asked the blacksmith, turning once more in his seat.

By this time they were within a few rods of the blacksmith's yard, and William became bold, now that he had nothing to lose by it.

"My name isn't Christopher," he answered in his usual tone.

"Your name isn't Christopher? That's what your uncle told me."

"I think you are mistaken," said William, quietly.

"What's got into the boy? Is he goin' to deny his own name? What is your name, then?"

"My name is William Morris," was the distinct response.

"What!" exclaimed the blacksmith, in amazement.

"I think you ought to know me, Mr. Bickford. I worked for you some time, you know."

"Take off your hat, and let me look at your face!" said Aaron Bickford, sternly.

William laughed as he complied with the request. It was now rather lighter, and the blacksmith, peering into his face, saw that it was indeed true—that the boy on the back seat was not Kit Watson at all, but his ex-apprentice, William Morris.

"It's Bill Morris, by the living jingo!" he exclaimed. "What do you say to that, Sarah?"

"You're a master hand at managing boys, Aaron," said his wife, sarcastically.

"How came you in the wagon, Bill Morris?" demanded Bickford, not caring to answer his wife.

"The giant put me in," answered William.

"Where is that boy, Christopher Watson?"

"I expect he is travelin' with the show, Mr. Bickford."

"Who put you up to this mean trick?" demanded the blacksmith, wrathfully.

"Kit Watson."

"I've got an account to settle with you, William Morris. I s'pose you think you've done something pretty smart."

"I think he has, Aaron," said Mrs. Bickford, who seemed to take a malicious pleasure in opening her husband's wounds afresh.

"Mrs. Bickford, it isn't very creditable in you to triumph

over your husband, just after he's been spendin' fifty cents for your amusement."

"Goodness knows, Mr. Bickford, you don't often take me to shows. I guess what you spend that way won't ruin you."

While the married pair were indulging in their little recriminations, William had managed to slip out of the wagon in the rear, and he was now a rod away.

"Good-night, Mr. Bickford!" he shouted. "I'm much obliged to you for bringing me home. It's saved me a long walk."

The blacksmith's reply was one that I do not care to record. He was thoroughly angry and disgusted. If it hadn't been so late he would have got out and tried to inflict punishment on William with his whip, but the boy was too far away by this time to make this possible.

CHAPTER XIX.

STEPHEN WATSON VISITS OAKFORD.

On Monday as Mr. Bickford was about his work a carriage drove into the yard containing Stephen Watson and Ralph. "Good-morning, Mr. Bickford," said Stephen Watson. "I've called over to inquire about Kit. I hope he is doing his duty by you."

The blacksmith looked at Mr. Watson with embarrassment, and did not immediately reply.

Mr. Watson repeated his question.

"Kit isn't with me," answered Bickford, at length.

"Isn't with you!" repeated Stephen Watson, in surprise. "Where is he?"

"He's run away."

"Run away!" ejaculated Kit's uncle. "What is the meaning of that?"

"He said he didn't want to be a blacksmith, and that you had no authority to make him."

"But where has he gone? Have you any idea?"

"He has gone off with Barlow's circus."

"But what object can he have in going off with a circus?" asked Mr. Watson, no less bewildered.

"They've hired him to perform."

"Are you sure of this?"

"I ought to be," answered the blacksmith, grimly. "My wife and I saw him jumpin' round last evenin' in the circus tent over at Grafton."

"But I don't see what he—a green hand—can do. Ralph, can you throw any light on this mystery?"

Ralph explained that Kit had practiced acrobatic feats extensively at the gymnasium connected with the school.

"Did he ever talk of going off with a circus?" asked Mr. Watson.

"Never, though he enjoyed the exercise."

"I went after him and tried to get him back," said Mr. Bickford, "but he gave me the slip."

"He's done a very foolish and crazy thing. He can't get more than three or four dollars a week from the circus, and in the fall he'll be out of a job."

"Just as you say, sir. He'd have a good payin' trade if he stayed with me. What do you think it is best to do about it, Mr. Watson?"

"I shall do nothing. If the boy chooses to make a fool of himself, he may try it. Next fall, and possibly before, he'll be coming back in rags, and beg me to take him back."

"I hope you won't take him back," said Ralph, who was jealous of Kit.

"I shall not consider myself bound to do so, but if he consents to obey me, and learn a trade of Mr. Bickford, I will fit him up, and enable him to do so—out of charity, and because he is my nephew."

"Then you don't mean to do anything about it, sir?" asked Aaron Bickford, considerably disappointed, for he longed to get Kit into his power once more.

"No, I will leave the boy to himself. Ralph, as our business seems to be over, we will turn about and go home."

Mr. Watson drove out of the blacksmith's yard.

"Well, Ralph," he said, as they were on their way home, "I am very much annoyed at what your cousin has done, but I don't see that I am to blame."

"Of course you're not, pa," returned Ralph, promptly.

"Still the public may misjudge me. It will be very awkward to answer questions about Kit. I really don't know what to say."

"Say he's run away and joined the circus. We might as well tell the truth."

"I don't know but it will be best. I will add that, though it grieves me, I think it advisable, as he is so old, not to interfere with him, but let him see the error of his way for himself. I will say also that when he chooses to come back, I will make suitable arrangements for him."

"I guess that will do. I will say the same."

"I don't mind saying to you that I shall feel it quite a relief to be rid of the expense of maintaining him, for he has cost me a great deal of money. You are my son, and of course I expect to take care of you, and bring you up as a gentleman, but he has no claim upon me except that of relationship. I won't say that to others, however."

"You are quite right, pa. As he is poor, and has his own

living to make, it isn't best to send him to a high-priced school, and give him too much money to spend."

It will be seen that there was a striking resemblance between the views of father and son, both of whom were intensely selfish, mean, and unscrupulous.

Stephen Watson foresaw that there would be a difficulty in making outside friends of the family understand why Kit had left home. He deliberately resolved to misrepresent him, and the opportunity came sooner than he anticipated.

On the afternoon of the day of his call upon the blacksmith, there was a ring at the bell, and a middle-aged stranger was ushered into the parlor.

"I suppose you don't remember me," he said to Stephen Watson.

"I can't say I do," replied Stephen, eying him closely.

"I knew your brother better than I did you. I am Harry Miller, who used to go to school with you both in the old red schoolhouse on the hill."

"I remember your name, but I should not have remembered you."

"I don't wonder. Time changes us all. I am sorry to hear that your poor brother is dead."

"Yes," answered Stephen, heaving a sigh proper to the occasion, which was intended to signify his grief at the loss. "He was cut down like the grass of the field. It is the common lot."

"His wife died earlier, did she not?"

"Yes."

"But there was a son?"

"Yes."

"How old is the boy?"

"Just turned sixteen."

"May I see him? I should like to see the son of my old deskmate."

"Ah!" sighed Stephen, "I wish he were here to meet you."

"But surely he is not dead?"

"No; he is not dead, but he is a source of anxiety to me."

"And why?" asked the visitor, with concern. "Has he turned out badly?"

"Why, I don't know that I can exactly say that he has turned out badly."

"What is the matter with him, then?"

"He is wayward, and instead of being willing to devote himself to his school studies like my son Ralph, he has formed an extraordinary taste for the circus."

"Indeed! but where is he?"

"He is traveling with Barlow's circus."

"In what capacity?"

"As an acrobat."

Henry Miller laughed.

"I remember," he said, "that his father was fond of athletic sports. You never were."

"No, I was a quiet boy."

"That you were, and uncommonly sly!" thought Miller, but he did not consider it polite to say so. "Is the boy—by the way, what is his name?"

"Christopher. He is generally called Kit."

"Well, is Kit a good gymnast?"

"I believe he is."

"When did he join the circus?"

"Only yesterday. In fact—it is painful for me to say so,—he ran away from a good home to associate with mountebanks."

"And what are you going to do about it?"

"He is so headstrong that I have thought it best to give him his own way, and let him see for himself how foolish he has been. Of course he has a home to return to whenever he sees fit."

"That may be the best way. I should like to see the young rascal. I would follow up the circus and do so, only I am unfortunately called to California on business. I am part owner of a gold mine out there."

"I trust you have been prospered in your worldly affairs."

"Yes, I have every reason to be thankful. I suppose I am worth two hundred thousand dollars."

Stephen Watson, whose god was money, almost turned green with jealousy. At the same time he asked himself how he could take advantage of his old schoolmate's good luck.

"I wish he would take a fancy to my Ralph," he thought.

So he called in Ralph, and introduced him to the rich stranger.

"He's a good boy, my Ralph," he said; "sober and correct in all his habits, and fond of school and study."

Ralph was rather surprised to hear this panegyric, but presently his father explained to him in private the object he had in view. Then Ralph made himself as agreeable as he could, but he failed to please Mr. Miller.

"He is too much like his father," he said to himself.

When he terminated his call, he received a very cordial invitation to come again on his return from California.

"If Kit has returned I certainly will come," he replied, an answer which pleased neither Ralph nor his father.

CHAPTER XX.

A CHAT WITH A CANDY BUTCHER.

KIT had a berth assigned him in one of the circus cars. His nearest neighbor was Harry Thorne, a young man of twenty-four, who filled the position of candy butcher. As this term may sound strange to my readers, I will explain that it is applied to the venders of candy, lemonade, peanuts, and other articles such as are patronized by those who come to see the show. It is really a very profitable business, as will be explained in the course of the story.

Harry Thorne was sociable and ready to give Kit any information about the circus.

"How long is it since you joined a circus?" asked Kit, after getting acquainted.

"I was younger than you," answered Thorne.

"Why did you join? What gave you the idea?"

"A spirit of adventure, I think. Besides, there was a large family of us—I am the oldest—and it was necessary for me to do something."

"That's a queer name—candy butcher."

"It seems so to you, but I am used to it."

"Did you become a candy butcher at once?"

"Not till I was eighteen. Before that I ran errands and made myself generally useful. I thought of being an acrobat, like you, but I was too stout and not active enough."

"I shouldn't think there would be much money made in your business," said Kit.

"That shows you don't know much about circus matters. Last fall I ran in with seven hundred dollars saved, besides paying all my expenses during the six months I was out."

"You ought to be pretty well off now, if you have been a candy butcher for five or six years."

"I haven't a cent, and am owing two hundred dollars in Philadelphia."

"How is that?"

"You don't often find a circus man that saves money. It's easy come, easy go. But I send money home every season— three or four hundred dollars at least, if I do well."

"That's a good thing, anyway. But if I were in your place I would put away some money every season."

"I could do it, but it's hard to make up my mind."

"I can't see how you can make such sums. It puzzles me."

"We are paid a fixed salary, say twenty-five dollars a month, and commission on sales. I was always pretty lucky in selling, and my income has sometimes been very large.

But I don't make much in large places. It is in the smaller towns that the money is made. When a country beau brings his girl to the circus, he don't mind expense. He makes up his mind to spend several dollars in having a good time—so he buys lemonade, peanuts, apples, and everything that he or his girl fancies. In the city, where there are plenty of places where such things can be bought, we don't sell much. In New York or Philadelphia I make very little more than my salary."

"What is there most profit on?" asked Kit.

"Well, I should say lemonade. You've heard of circus lemonade?"

"Is there anything peculiar about it?"

"Yes, something peculiarly weak. A good-sized lemon will make half a dozen glasses, and perhaps more. But there is something cheaper still, and that is citric acid. I remember one hot day in an Ohio town. The thermometer stood at 99 degrees and there wasn't a drop of spring or well water to be had, for we had cornered it. All who were thirsty had to drink lemonade, and it took a good many glasses to quench thirst. I made a harvest that day, and so did the other candy butchers. If we could have a whole summer of such days, I could retire on a small fortune in October."

"Do you like the circus business?"

"Sometimes I get tired of it, but when the spring opens I generally have the circus fever."

"What do you do in the winter?"

"It is seldom I get anything to do. I am an expense, and that is why I find myself in debt when the new season opens. Last winter I was more lucky. A young fellow—an old circus acquaintance of mine—has a store in the country, and he offered to supply me with a stock of goods to sell on commission in country villages near by. In that way I filled up about three months, making my expenses, but doing nothing more. However, that was a great thing for me, and I start this season only two hundred dollars in debt, as I think I told you a few minutes ago."

"Is it the same way with performers?"

"No; they have a better chance. Next winter, if you try, you can probably make an engagement to perform at some dime museum or variety hall, in New York or elsewhere. I once got the position of ticket-seller for a part of the winter."

"I don't think I should like to perform in a dime museum," said Kit.

"What's the odds, if you are well paid for it?"

"I don't intend to make my present business a permanent one."

"That's different. What will you do next fall?"

"I may go to school."

Harry Thorne whistled.

"That will be a novelty," he said. "I haven't been to school since I was twelve years old."

"Wouldn't you like to go now?"

"No; I'm too old. Are you much of a scholar?"

"I'm a pretty good Latin scholar, and know something of Greek."

"I'll bet there isn't another acrobat in the country that can say that. What salary do you get, if you don't mind telling?"

"Twenty-five dollars a week."

"You're in luck. How came Barlow to give you so much?"

"I think he took a liking to me. Perhaps he wanted to pay me for facing the lion at Smyrna."

"Were you the boy who did that? I thought your face looked familiar. You've got pluck, Kit."

"I hope so; but I'm not sure whether it is I or the snuff that is entitled to the most credit."

"Anyhow it took some courage, even if you did have the snuff with you."

"Do you know what is to be our route this season?"

"I think we are going West as far as St. Louis, taking all the larger towns and cities on our way. We are to show a week in Chicago. But I don't care so much for the cities as the country towns—the one-night places."

"Does Mr. Barlow go with us?"

"Not steadily. He drops in on us here and there. There's one thing I can say for him—he won't have any man in his employ drink or gamble. We have to bind ourselves to total abstinence while we are in his employ—that is, till the end of the season. Gambling is the great vice of circus men; it is more prevalent even than drinking."

"Don't the men do it on the sly?"

"They run a risk if they do. At the first offense they are fined, at the second or third they are bounced."

"That doesn't trouble me any. I neither drink nor gamble."

"Good for you."

"Say, when are you two fellows goin' to stop talkin'?" was heard from a neighboring berth. "You don't give a fellow a chance to sleep."

Kit and his new friend took the hint and addressed themselves to slumber.

CHAPTER XXI.

KIT MEETS A SCHOOLMATE.

KIT slept profoundly, being very tired. He was taken by surprise when, the next morning, he was shaken into a state of wakefulness, and opening his eyes met those of his neighbor Harry Thorne.

"Is it morning?" he asked, in a sleepy tone.

"I should say it was. It is a quarter after nine, and the parade starts at ten."

"The parade?"

"Yes; we give a morning parade in every place we visit. If you are not on hand to take part in it, you will be fined five dollars."

"I'll be up in a jiffy," said Kit, springing out of his berth. "But there's time enough, isn't there?"

"Yes; but not too much. You will want to get some breakfast. By the way, are you used to driving?"

"Oh, yes. I have done a good deal of it," answered Kit.

"I thought so, as you are a country boy. How would you like to drive a span of horses attached to one of the small chariots?"

Kit was extremely fond of a horse, and he answered promptly, "I'll do it."

"There are two. The other is driven by Charlie Davis, once a performer but now a ticket man. He is a little older than you."

"All right. I don't see how I came to sleep so late."

"You and Charlie are good matches. Once he went to bed Saturday night, and did not wake up till Monday morning."

"That beats my record!"

Kit was dressed in less than ten minutes.

"Where shall I get breakfast?" he asked.

"The regular breakfast is over, and you will have to buy some. There is a restaurant just opposite the lot. You might get in with one of the cooks, and get something in the cook tent."

"No; I'll go to the restaurant. To-morrow I'll be on hand at the regular breakfast."

The restaurant was a small one, with no pretensions to style, but Kit was hungry and not particular. At the same table there was a dark-complexioned boy of about his own size, who had just begun to dispatch a beefsteak.

He looked up as Kit seated himself.

"You're the new acrobat, are you not?" asked the other.

"Yes; are you Charlie Davis?"

"Yes; how do you know me?"

"Harry Thorne was speaking of you."

"I see you're one of the late birds as well as I. I generally have to buy my breakfast outside. How do you like circus life?"

"I haven't tried it well enough to tell. This is only my second day."

"I went into it at fourteen. I've been an acrobat, too, but I have a weak ankle, and have gone into the ticket department."

"Are you going to remain in the circus permanently?"

"No, I'm trying to wean myself from it. A friend has promised to set me up in business whenever I get ready to retire. If I kept on, I would be no better off at forty than I am now."

"Yet circus people make a good deal of money, I hear."

"Right you are, my boy, but they don't keep it. They get spoiled for anything else, and sooner or later they are left out in the cold. I've had a good deal of fun out of it, for I like traveling, but I'm going to give it up."

"I took it up because I had nothing else to do, but I shan't stay in it long. I'll tell you about it some day. I hear you drive one of the pony chariots."

"Yes."

"I am to drive the other."

"Good! Don't let them run away with you, my boy."

"I'll try not to," said Kit, smiling. "Is there any danger?"

"Not much. They're trained. Are you fond of horses?"

"I like nothing better."

"So it is with me. I'll wait till you are through breakfast, and then we'll go over together."

Half an hour later Kit sat on the box of a chariot, drawn by two beautiful ponies. The circus line had been formed, and the parade began. Behind him was a circus wagon, or rather a cage on wheels, through the gratings of which could be seen a tiger, crafty and cruel-looking. In front was an elephant, with two or three performers on his back. Kit was dressed in street costume, his circus dress not being required.

In another part of the procession was Charlie Davis, driving a corresponding wagon.

Kit felt a peculiar exhilaration as he drove his ponies, and reflected upon the strangeness of his position, as compared with his previous experiences. He had from time to time watched circus processions, but not in his wildest and most improbable dreams had it ever occurred to him to imagine that he would ever himself take part in one. As he looked down from his perch he saw the streets lined with the usual curious crowd of spectators, among whom boys were largely represented.

"I suppose some of them are envying me," he thought to himself, with a smile. "Suppose there was someone who recognized me?"

No sooner had the thought come into his mind, than he heard his own name called in a voice indicating amazement.

"Kit Watson, by all that's wonderful!" were the words that fell on his ears.

Looking to the right, his glance fell upon Jack Dormer, a schoolmate, who had been attending the same academy with him for a year past.

Kit colored, feeling a little embarrassed.

"How are you, Jack?" he said.

"How came you to be in this circus procession, Kit?"

"I can't tell you now. Come round to the lot, after the parade is over, and I'll tell you all about it."

Jack availed himself of the invitation and presented himself at the circus grounds.

"What does it all mean, Kit?" he asked. "Have you really and truly joined the circus?"

"Come round this afternoon, and you'll see me perform. I am one of the Vincenti brothers, acrobats."

"But what put it in your head? That's what I want to know?"

"I thought I would like it better than being a blacksmith."

"But who ever dreamed of your being a blacksmith?"

"My uncle did. I'll tell you all about it."

Kit told his story. Jack Dormer listened with sympathetic interest.

"Do they pay you well?" he asked.

"I get twenty-five dollars a week, and all expenses."

"Can you get me a job?" asked Jack, quite overcome by the magnificence of the salary.

"As an acrobat, Jack?" asked Kit, laughing, for Jack had the reputation of being one of the clumsiest boys in school.

"Well, no, I don't suppose I could do much in that way, but isn't there something I could do?"

"Take my advice, Jack, and give it up. You've got a good home, and there is no need of your going into any such business even if you were qualified."

"Don't you like it?"

"I can't tell yet. Of course it is exciting, but those who have been in it a good while advise against it. I may not stay in it any more than one season."

"Shall I tell the fellows at school where you are?"

"No, I would rather you wouldn't."

"Does your cousin Ralph come back to school?"

"Yes."

"We could spare him a good deal better than you."

"I am not fond of Ralph myself, but the world is wide enough for us both."

Kit saw his schoolmate again after the afternoon performance, and received many compliments.

"I couldn't believe it was you," he said. "You acted as if you were an old hand at the business."

CHAPTER XXII.

NEW ACQUAINTANCES.

SUNDAY was of course a day of rest for the circus employees. Most of them observed it by lying in bed unusually late. Kit, however, rose in good season, and found himself first at breakfast. When the proper time arrived, he walked to the village, and selecting the first church he came to, entered. He had always been in the habit of attending church, and felt that there was no good reason why he should give up the practice now that he was away from home.

He stood in the lobby, waiting for the sexton to appear, when a fine-looking man of middle age entered the church with a young girl of fourteen at his side.

He glanced at Kit with interest, and after a moment's pause he walked up to him.

"Are you a stranger here?" he asked.

"Yes, sir," answered Kit.

"I shall be glad to have you accept a seat in my pew."

"Thank you, sir," said Kit, politely; "I was waiting for the sexton, intending to ask him for a seat."

"I have plenty of room in my pew, having only my daughter with me. Are you staying long in the town?"

"Only as long as the circus does," answered Kit.

The gentleman looked surprised.

"Are you connected with the circus?" he asked, quickly.

"Yes, sir."

By this time the young girl was examining Kit with interest and attention.

"Is it possible you are a performer?"

"Yes, sir."

"I wouldn't have dreamed it. You look like a young gentleman."

"I hope I am, sir."

"Pardon me, I meant no offense, but you don't at all answer my idea of a circus performer."

"I have only been two days with the circus," said Kit; "and that may account for my not having a circus look."

"It is time to take our seats. I will speak with you afterwards. First, however, let me introduce my daughter, Evelyn Grant."

"I am glad to make your acquaintance, Miss Evelyn," said Kit, removing his hat. "My name is Christopher Watson."

Evelyn offered her hand with a smile.

"I had no idea circus young men were so polite," she said.

There was no chance for any further conversation, as they had entered the church. Mr. Grant's pew was in a prominent position. He drew back to let the two young people enter. They seated themselves at the lower end of the pew and Mr. Grant took his seat at the head. Kit noticed that several persons in neighboring pews regarded him with apparent curiosity.

Kit enjoyed the services, which were of an interesting character. He had expected to feel like a stranger, but thanks to the kindness of Mr. Grant he felt quite as much at home as when he sat in his uncle's pew at Smyrna.

When the services were over, they filed slowly out of church. A new surprise was in store for Kit.

"If you have no engagement we shall be glad to have you dine with us, Master Watson," said Mr. Grant.

"You will come, won't you?" said Evelyn, with a smile.

"You are very kind," said Kit, in grateful surprise. "Nothing would be more agreeable to me."

Just then a gentleman approached Mr. Grant, and said: "I am glad to see you looking so well, Mr. Mayor."

"Is your father the mayor of the city?" asked Kit.

"Yes; he was elected last December."

"I am very fortunate to be invited to dinner by the mayor."

"And by the mayor's daughter. Don't forget that."

"You may be sure I appreciate that, too."

"How funny it seems to me to be walking with a circus performer! What do you do? You don't stand upon a horse's back, and jump through hoops, do you?"

"No, I can't do that."

"But what do you do?"

"I am an acrobat."

Kit explained to her what he did.

"It must be very hard."

"Oh, no! I learned to do it in a gymnasium, before I ever dreamed of being connected with a circus."

"Where was the gymnasium?"

"Attached to Dr. Codman's academy."

"Why, I have a cousin who attended there," said Evelyn, in surprise.

"What is his name?"

"Edward Moore."

"I know him very well. He is a nice fellow."

At this moment Kit, in looking around, was surprised to see the familiar face and figure of Mr. Barlow, the circus proprietor, who had evidently, like himself, been attending the service. Recognition was mutual.

"I am glad to see you here, Watson," said **Mr. Barlow,**
offering his hand. "I always attend church myself when
I have an opportunity, but I'm afraid few of my employ
follow my example. I always feel more confidence in any
young man who seems to enjoy a church service."

Mr. Barlow was a man whose name was widely known,
and Kit saw that Mr. Grant looked as if he would like to
be introduced.

"Mr. Barlow," he said, "allow me to introduce a new
friend, Mr. Grant, who is the mayor of the town."

"I am pleased to make your acquaintance, Mr. Mayor,"
said the showman, offering his hand.

"The pleasure is mutual, sir," said the mayor. "I need
not say that your name has long been familiar to me."

"I am glad you have taken one of my young men under
your wing. He is a recent acquisition, but I have reason
to think well of him."

"He is to dine with us to-day. I shall be glad to extend
an invitation to you also, Mr. Barlow."

"You are very kind, and but for a previous engagement
I would accept with pleasure. I shall be glad to see you at
my show to-morrow with complimentary tickets."

"What a nice old gentleman Mr. Barlow is," said Evelyn,
in a low voice.

"I have found him an excellent friend. He won't allow
any of us to drink or gamble while we are in his employ."

"I hope you wouldn't want to do either, Mr. Watson."

"I have no disposition to do so. But, Miss Evelyn, I want
to ask you a favor."

"What is it? If it isn't anything very great, I may
grant it."

"Don't call me Mr. Watson."

"What shall I call you, then?"

"My friends call me Kit."

"That's a nice name. Yes, I'll call you Kit."

It will be seen that the two young people were getting
on famously.

"Do you live far away, Miss Evelyn?"

"About a quarter of a mile from here."

In turning the corner of a street, Kit met his friend Harry
Thorne, walking with Charlie Davis. Both regarded Kit
with surprise.

"Kit seems to be getting on," said Charlie. "Do you know
who he is walking with?"

"No; do you?"

"With the daughter of the mayor."

"How do you know?"

"The gentleman in front was pointed out to me as the
mayor. I shouldn't wonder if he were going to dine there."

When Kit returned to the circus tent about four o'clock

in the afternoon, he met with some good-natured raillery which he took in good part. He felt that he had passed the day in a much more satisfactory manner than if, like the great majority of his companions, he had risen late and lounged about the circus grounds, beguiling the time with smoking and story-telling.

CHAPTER XXIII.

KIT'S DARING ACT.

KIT'S acts thus far had been confined to the ring, but now a new one was expected from him. Early in the performance a series of flying leaps from a springboard, in which all the acrobats took part, was introduced. From a point thirty feet back the performer ran swiftly till he reached the springboard, from which a leap was made accompanied by a somersault, carrying him over a considerable space in advance.

It was the custom to place first one elephant, then a second, and finally a third, in front of the springboard. There was only one man who could leap over three elephants. The two Vincenti brothers took part regularly, but Kit, being a new hand, had thus far been excused. But one of the regular performers being temporarily unwell, it was considered desirable that his place should be supplied.

"Do you think you can do it?" asked Alonzo Vincenti, somewhat doubtfully.

"Yes," answered Kit, confidently.

"It will be sufficient if you jump over one elephant," continued his associate. "Then you can drop out."

"I can do better than that," said Kit.

"I don't know about that. My brother can only jump over two."

"You jump over three elephants?"

"Yes; but I am the only one who can do it. It takes a good spring to clear even two. It won't do to lose your head."

"Can I have a chance to rehearse?"

"Yes, I will speak about it."

"Then I will appear this evening."

"But if you fail you are likely to hurt yourself."

"I know that. That is why I would rather make the first trial in the evening. The lights and the crowd will excite and help me."

Kit was not foolhardy in his undertaking, for he had already had some practice in similar feats with his old teacher. Besides, he was ambitious. In school his ambition had shown itself in his attempt to eclipse his schoolfellows in scholarship. In the gymnasium he had ranked first, and now that he had joined the circus he didn't like to be assigned to a place in the rear.

Let me take the opportunity here to advise my young readers not to imitate Kit in essaying dangerous parts. "Be bold, but not too bold!" is a very good motto.

During the afternoon Kit found an opportunity to practice in the empty tent, in order to settle the question whether he had lost any of his old-time skill. The result was satisfactory, and renewed his confidence.

"I can do better before a tent full of spectators than when practicing by myself," he decided.

The evening came.

Standing near the ticket-seller half an hour before the show began, Kit heard his name called.

Turning quickly he saw his friends of the previous day, Mayor Grant and his daughter Evelyn.

"Good-evening, my boy!" said the mayor, cordially. "We have come to see what you can do."

"Then I hope I shall do myself credit," said Kit, shaking hands with the mayor and his daughter. "Have you engaged seats?"

"Not yet."

"Then let me select them for you."

"With pleasure. I am glad to have a friend at court."

Kit selected seats as near as possible to the ring where he was to perform.

"These are splendid seats," said Evelyn. "How soon do you appear?"

"In a few minutes. I shall have to leave you now, but I will be back after my first act."

"What a nice boy he is, papa!" said Evelyn.

"Yes; it is a pity he is attached to a circus."

"Why? Isn't it a respectable business?"

"Yes; but there are many temptations connected with it, and most circus performers never rise any higher."

Evelyn was not inclined to discuss the question, though there is no doubt that she took a more favorable view of the circus profession than her father. The procession had just begun to move round the inner ring of the circus, including the elephants, the riders, the clowns, and performers of all kinds. Kit appeared, as in the public procession, driving a span of ponies.

This was the introduction. Then the various parts of the programme succeeded. Soon Kit performed his act in the ring. He had a new act to-night. Standing on the shoulders of one of the Vincenti brothers, he turned a somersault and landed on the shoulders of the other, standing six to eight feet away.

"I don't see how he does it, papa," said Evelyn. "He must be very smart."

"I see you are determined to make a hero of this young man, Evelyn."

"Don't you admire him yourself, papa?"

"Admire is rather a strong word, daughter. I will admit, however, that I like him, and hope he will soon change his business."

After the act was over, Kit came round and received congratulations. Evelyn repeated what her father said.

"I agree with you, sir," said Kit. "I haven't selected this as my life business, but shall keep my engagement till the end of the season."

"How, on the whole, do you like your new associates? I don't need to be told that they are very different from those to whom you are accustomed."

"They are very kind to me, and generous to each other when there is need. They will divide their last dollar with a friend."

"They often come to their last dollar, don't they?"

"Yes; they can't keep money. They are always in debt when the new season opens, no matter how much they brought home with them at the end of the last."

"Are there no exceptions?"

"Yes, a few. I have heard of one circus manager who commenced as a candy butcher, and now is proprietor of a very fair-sized show. Of course he had to save up money, or he would never have succeeded so well."

Kit had to cut short his visit, for the new act, already referred to, was near at hand.

In the list of leapers Kit came last. First of all, there was a simple somersault from the springboard. This was easy. Just after Kit came the clown, who, though really a clever acrobat, stopped short when he came to the board and merely jumped up and down to the amusement of the young spectators.

"He can't jump no more'n I can," said one small boy, contemptuously.

"I shouldn't think they'd let him try," said another.

Both boys were surprised when, in the next trial, where the task was to jump over an elephant, the despised clown made a good spring and landed fairly on his feet.

"I guess he was afraid before," said the first boy.

"No; he only pretended for fun. Do you see that boy? I wonder if he can jump over the elephant."

The question was soon answered. Kit took his turn and sprang with apparent ease over the great beast.

Next another elephant was driven in alongside of the first. Again the leapers advanced to try their skill. But two held back, not feeling competent for the task. The clown once more made a feint of jumping, but only jumped up and retired, apparently filled with confusion.

Evelyn gazed in intense excitement.

"It must be awfully hard to jump like that, papa," she said.

"I don't think I shall ever try it, Evelyn."

Another elephant was driven alongside the other two, making three in all. The other contestants retired, for only Alonzo had succeeded hitherto in executing this difficult feat. He expected to be the only one now, but noticed with surprise that Kit seemed ready to follow him.

"You don't mean to try it, Kit?" he said, in amazement.

"Why not?"

"You will fail, and if you do, you may hurt yourself seriously."

"I shall not fail," said Kit, confidently.

Alonzo looked anxious, but there was no time to expostulate. He ran swiftly to the board, made a vigorous spring, and landed handsomely on the bedding which had been provided beyond. He had scarcely stepped aside, when, to the astonishment of the other acrobats, Kit gathered himself up, ran to the springboard, and exerting himself to the utmost, made his leap, and landed a foot ahead of Alonzo.

Then the tent rang with applause, and there were many exclamations of astonishment, not only among the spectators, but also among the circus performers.

Kit's face flushed with pleasure, and bowing his acknowledgments, he withdrew.

"He is certainly a wonderful boy," said the mayor.

CHAPTER XXIV.

KIT RECEIVES A LETTER.

Kit received compliments enough to spoil him, if he had not been a strong-minded and level-headed boy. Among others Mr. Barlow, who had been present and witnessed his daring act, took the opportunity to congratulate him.

"You seem to be born for a circus performer, my young friend," he said. "You have come to the front at once."

"Thank you, sir," said Kit. "I am glad that I succeeded, but such success as that does not satisfy my ambition."

"You mean, perhaps, that you want to jump over four, perhaps five elephants?" suggested the manager.

Kit smiled.

"No," he answered; "I don't think I shall venture beyond

three. But I don't expect to remain in the circus more than this season."

"That is almost a pity, when you are so well qualified to excel in it."

"Mr. Barlow," said Kit, seriously, "if I were a great manager like you, I would not mind, but I don't care to go through life as a circus performer."

"I don't know but you are right, my boy. In fact I know you are. I shouldn't care to be a performer myself."

"I don't think you would excel in that line," said Kit, with a glance at the portly form of the well-known showman.

"You wouldn't advise me to try jumping over elephants, I infer," said Mr. Barlow, with an amused smile.

"No, sir."

"I will take your advice, my boy. Though your share of worldly experience isn't great, you are certainly correct in that. I shall relieve the fears of Mrs. Barlow at once by telling her that I have decided not to enter the ring."

Kit also received the congratulations of the mayor and Evelyn, but the former added: "Though your act was a daring one, I was almost sorry to see it."

"Why, sir?"

"I feared it would confirm you in your love of your present business."

"No, sir, there is no danger," replied Kit. "I have a fair education already, and prefer to qualify myself for something different."

"I am glad to hear you say so. You are undoubtedly right."

"I must say good-by now," said Kit; "for we get off at midnight."

"Shall you not return this way?"

"No, sir; we are to go West, I hear."

"I hope when the season is over, you will make us a visit. Come and stay a week," said the mayor, hospitably.

"Do come," said Evelyn, earnestly.

"How can I thank you for your kindness to a stranger?" said Kit, gratefully. "I shall certainly avail myself of your hospitality. There are not many who would take such notice of a circus boy."

"You are something more than a circus boy," said the mayor, "or I might not have been so drawn to you. Good-by, then, and if you ever need a friend, don't forget that you are at liberty to call upon me."

It was a source of regret to Kit that he was obliged to part with friends whom in so short a time he had come to value so highly. He resolved that he would accept the mayor's offer at the close of the season. He would need a friend and adviser, and he felt confident that Mayor Grant's counsel would be wise and judicious.

Kit was already asleep in his bunk when the circus train started for the next place on the route. When he woke up he was in the town of Colebrook. Here a surprise was in store for him in the shape of a letter from his uncle. When he saw the familiar handwriting and the postmark "Smyrna," he broke the seal with a feeling of curiosity. He did not expect to derive either pleasure or satisfaction from the perusal.

We will look over his shoulder while he is reading the letter.

"NEPHEW CHRISTOPHER: I cannot express to you my surprise and disappointment when I rode over to Oakford to see you, and learned from Mr. Bickford that you had run away from his house and joined the circus. There must be something low and depraved in your tastes, that you should thus abandon the prospect of earning a respectable livelihood, and go tramping through the country with a circus. What do you think your father would say if he could come to life, and become aware of the course you have so rashly taken?

"I should be justified in forcibly removing you from your present associations, and returning you to your worthy employer, Mr. Aaron Bickford, and perhaps it is my duty to do so. But I think it wiser for you to realize for yourself the folly of your course. You have deliberately deserted a good home and a kind guardian and become a tramp, if I may so express myself. I cannot imagine my son Ralph doing such a thing. He is, I hope, too dutiful and too sensible to throw away the advantages which fortune has secured him, to become a mountebank.

"It is very embarrassing to me to answer questions about you. There are some who will be unjust enough, I doubt not, to blame me for your wild course, but I shall be sustained by the consciousness of my entire innocence in the matter. At great expense I have maintained you and paid the cost of your education, giving you privileges and advantages equal to those I have given my own boy. I have done so cheerfully, because you were my nephew, and I am sorry you have made me so poor a return. But I shall look for my reward to my own conscience, and hope you may yet see the folly and wickedness of your course.

"I have only to add that when that time comes you are welcome to return to my roof and protection, and I will intercede with your excellent employer, Mr. Bickford, to take you back and teach you his trade, whereby you may be enabled to earn a more respectable living than you are doing at present. Ralph joins me in this wish.

"Your uncle,
"STEPHEN WATSON."

Kit's lip curled when he read this hypocritical letter, and he was tempted to despise his uncle more now than ever. He lost no time in sending this reply:

"UNCLE STEPHEN: I have received your letter, and can only express my surprise at the view you take of your treatment of me. Whether my father really left me as destitute as you claim, I am not in a position to say. If you have really gone to personal expense in maintaining and educating me up to this point, I shall, when I am able, reimburse you to the last cent. But I cannot forgive you for your trying to force a boy, reared and educated as I have been, to learn the trade of a blacksmith. You say that I have enjoyed advantages similar to those of your son Ralph. I wish to ask whether you would dream of apprenticing him to any such business.

"You speak of my low associations, and call me a mountebank.. In the town I have just left I was the guest of the mayor, and have promised to spend a week at his house on a visit when the circus season is over. Though you have done your best to lower me socially, I am confident that I shall be able to win a good place by my own unaided exertions.

"I have no intention of continuing as a circus performer, though I am very liberally paid. It is too soon for me to decide upon my future course, but you may tell Mr. Bickford he need not wait for me to resume my place in his shop.

"I do not know when I shall see you or Ralph again, but you need have no fear that I shall appeal to your generosity.
"Your nephew,
"CHRISTOPHER WATSON."

Stephen Watson read this letter with surprise and chagrin. He was sorry to hear that Kit was doing so well, and alarmed at his implied doubt whether he had really been left destitute by his father.

"That boy is going to give me trouble," he muttered.

CHAPTER XXV.

THE ATTACK ON THE CIRCUS TENT.

FOUR weeks passed, in which Kit continued to acquit himself to the satisfaction of the manager. His youth and pleasant face, added to his uncommon skill, made him a favorite with the public, and being a boy with a love of adventure, he enjoyed thoroughly the constant variety of circus life and travel.

All circus existence is not sunshine, however. There are communities which are always dreaded by circus managers, on account of the rough and lawless element which dominates them.

Early one morning Barlow's circus arrived at the mining town of Coalville (as we will call it), in Pennsylvania. An afternoon performance was given, and passed off smoothly; but in the evening a gang of about twenty miners made their appearance, bent on mischief.

Mr. Clark, the manager, sought Mr. Barlow.

" I think we shall have trouble this evening, Mr. Barlow," he said.

" Guard against it, then. What indications have you seen? "

" A gang of twenty miners have just entered the lot. They look ugly."

" Have the canvas men on guard, and summon the razor-backs, if necessary. Don't provoke a conflict, but be ready for one."

Mr. Clark hastily made his arrangements as quietly as possible. Near the ticket-seller lounged a body of men, strong and muscular.

These were the canvas men. Some of them looked as reckless and dangerous as the miners from whom a disturbance was feared.

These canvas men, whose duty it is to set up and take down the tents, are, for the most part, a rough set. They are paid from fifteen to twenty dollars a month and board. Their accommodations are very poor, but as good perhaps as they are accustomed to. They are not averse to a scrimmage, and obeyed with alacrity the directions of Mr. Clark.

The body of miners marched in procession to the ticket-seller and then halted, one serving as spokesman.

" Give us twenty tickets, boss," said the leader.

" Where is your money? " asked the ticket-seller, cautiously.

" Never you mind! We're on the free list, ain't we, boys? "

" Yes, we are! " was the chorus from his followers.

" There are no deadheads admitted to the show," said the ticket man, firmly.

" You'll be a deadhead yourself if you ain't careful, young feller! " was the retort.

" Keep back, men! There are others waiting for a chance to buy tickets."

" Let 'em wait! Just hand over them tickets, or we'll run over you."

The fellow looked so dangerous that the ticket-seller saw there was no time to parley.

He raised the well-known circus cry, which is called out in times of danger, like a summons to arms, "Hey, Rube!"

Instantly the canvas men and razorbacks rushed to the rescue, and made an impetuous attack on the disorderly crowd of miners. They, too, were aching for a fight, and there was a wild scene of battle, in which, as in the ancient days, the opposing forces fought hand to hand.

The canvas men were strong, but so were the miners. Their muscles were toughened by daily toil, and it looked as if the outsiders might win.

Kit was not of course called upon to take part in the contest, but he was unwillingly involved.

One of the miners detached himself from the main body, and creeping stealthily to the big tent, whipped out a large knife, and was on the point of cutting one of the ropes, his intention being to sever one after another till the big tent collapsed. Kit saw his design, and rushing forward, seized his arm.

"Hold on there!" he cried. "What are you about?"

"Let me alone, and mind your own business!" returned the miner, in a hoarse, deep voice.

But Kit saw that it was a critical moment, and that great mischief might be done. He looked about him for help, for he was far from able to cope with his brawny antagonist. Still he clung to the arm of the intruder, and succeeded in delaying his purpose.

"Let go or I'll cut you!" said the miner, savagely.

Then Kit in desperation raised the cry, "Hey, Rube!"

But it hardly seemed likely to bring the needed assistance, for all the fighting men were engaged in the battle near the ticket-seller.

"That won't do no good, young bantam!" said the ruffian, as he aimed a blow at our hero.

Kit's career would in all probability have been cut short, but for the timely arrival of Achilles Henderson. The giant had heard the boy's warning cry, and being near at hand, rushed to his aid. His arrival was most opportune. He seized the miner in his powerful grasp, and the ruffian, strong and muscular as he was, was like a child in his clutch. His knife fell from his hand, and he was shaken like a reed by the giant.

"Secure the knife, Kit!" cried Achilles.

Kit needed no second bidding. He stooped swiftly and took up the weapon.

But Achilles was needed in another direction.

The contest between the miners and the canvas men still raged fiercely near the ticket stand. It looked as if the intruders would conquer. From the ranks of the defenders rose a wild and desperate cry, "Hey, Rube!"

Achilles heard it.

"Come, Kit!" he said. "We are wanted."

He hurled the miner in his grasp to the ground with such force that the man lay senseless; then he rushed with all the speed which his long limbs enabled him to attain to the scene of the conflict.

Here again he was none too soon. The leader of the miners, who had been the first spokesman and aggressor, was armed with a powerful club with which he was preparing to deal the ticket-seller a terrible and possibly fatal blow, when Achilles rushed into the *melee* like a hurricane. He snatched the club from the hands of the ruffian, and dealt about him unsparingly.

The ringleader was the first to fall. Next Achilles attacked the rest of the brutal gang, till half a dozen men with broken heads lay upon the ground. The attacking force was completely demoralized, and in dismay fled from the field.

The ticket-seller breathed a sigh of relief.

"I thought I was done for, Mr. Henderson," he said, when the giant returned, flushed with his exertions. "You are equal to half a dozen men."

"I haven't had so much exercise in a long time," said Achilles, panting. "Kit, where is the knife that scalawag was going to cut the rope with?"

"Here it is, Mr. Henderson?"

"I will keep it in remembrance of this little adventure. Perhaps I had better go and look after the original owner."

He met the ruffian limping like one disabled. His look was sullen and menacing.

"Give me my knife," he growled.

"I couldn't think of it, my man!" said Achilles, blandly. "Evidently you are not old enough to be trusted with a knife."

"I'd like to thrash you!" growled the miner again.

"I've no doubt of it, my friend; your intentions are good, but can't be carried out. And now I have a word to say," he continued, sternly. "Just get out of the lot as fast as your legs can carry you, or I'll serve you worse than I did before."

The ruffian looked toward the ticket stand. He saw several of his friends limping away like himself, looking like whipped curs, and he saw that there was no choice for him but to obey. With a muttered oath and a sullen scowl, he left the grounds.

"Kit," said the giant, "it won't do for me to exercise like this every day. I shall need a second supper."

"You are certainly entitled to one, Mr. Henderson," replied our hero.

CHAPTER XXVI.

KIT IS MADE A PRISONER.

IT had been a day of exciting adventure, but so far as Kit was concerned the end was not yet. He performed as usual, but as his second act was over at quarter past nine, he thought, being fatigued, that he would not wait until the close, but go at once to the circus car in which he had a berth, and go to bed.

He crossed the lot, and emerged into the street.

It was moderately dark, there being no moon, and only the light of a few stars to relieve the gloom.

Kit had not taken a dozen steps from the lot when two stout men approached him, both evidently miners.

"That's the kid that prevented my cutting the rope," he heard one say.

"Is he? I saw him with the giant."

"I mean to settle his hash for him," said the first.

Kit saw that he was in danger, and turned to run back to his friends. But it was too late! The first speaker laid a strong arm upon his shoulder, and his boyish strength was not able to overcome it.

"Don't be in such a hurry, kid," said his captor.

"Let me go!" cried Kit.

"You belong to the circus, don't you?"

"Yes."

"What do you do?"

"I am an acrobat."

"What's that?"

"I leap and turn somersaults, and so on."

"Yes, I know. Do you remember me?"

"I might if it were lighter."

The man lit a match and held it close to his face.

"Do you know me now?"

"Yes."

"Who am I?"

"You are the man who tried to cut the ropes of the tent."

"Right you are. I would have succeeded but for you."

"I suppose you would."

"Did you call that giant to pitch into me?"

"No; I didn't know he was near."

"He treated me like a brute," said the man, wrathfully. "My limbs are aching now from the fall he gave me."

Kit did not answer.

"I'd like to give him a broken head, as he gave some of my friends. Where is he?"

"I suppose he is somewhere in the lot. I'll go and call him, if you want me to."

"That's too thin! Now I've got you I won't let you off so easy."

"What do you intend to do?" asked Kit, becoming alarmed.

"To give you a lesson."

Kit did not ask what kind of a lesson was meant, but he feared it included bodily injury. Then at least, if never before, he wished himself back at his uncle's house in Smyrna, uncongenial as it was otherwise.

The first speaker spoke in a low voice to the second. Kit did not hear the words, but judged what they were from what followed.

The two men placed him beside them, and he was sternly ordered to move on.

They kept the road for perhaps half a mile, then turned off into a narrow lane which appeared to ascend a hill. Finally they stopped in front of a dark cabin, of one story, which seemed to be unoccupied. The outer door was fastened by a bolt.

One of the men drew out a bolt, and threw open the door. A dark interior was revealed. One of the men lit a match, throwing a fitful light upon an empty room. At one end of the apartment was a ring, fixed in a beam, and in the corner was a stout rope.

"That will do," said the first speaker.

He took the rope, secured one end of it to the ring, and then tied Kit firmly with the balance. It was long enough to allow of his lying down.

"Now," said the first man, grimly, "I reckon the kid will be safe here till to-morrow."

They prepared to leave the cabin.

"Are you going to leave me here?" asked Kit, in dismay.

"Yes."

"What good will it do you?"

"You'll see—to-morrow."

Kit had ten dollars in his pocket, and he thought of offering it in return for his freedom, but it occurred to him fortunately that his captors would deprive him of it, as it was quite within their power to do, and not compensate him in any way. He understood by this time the character of the men into whose hands he had fallen, and he thought it prudent to remain silent.

As the first captor stood with the door open, while just on the point of leaving, he said, grimly, "How do you like it, kid?"

"Not at all," answered Kit.

"If you beg my pardon for what you did, I might let you go."

Kit did not believe this, and he had no intention of humiliating himself for nothing.

"I only did my duty," he said. "I have nothing to ask pardon for."

"You may change your mind—to-morrow!"

Another ominous reference to to-morrow. Evidently he was only deferring his vengeance, and intended to wreak it on his young prisoner the next day.

It was not a comforting thought, nor was it calculated to soothe Kit, weary as he was, to sleep.

The door was closed, and Kit heard the sliding of the bolt on the outside. He was a prisoner, securely enough, and with small chance of rescue.

Now, though Kit is my hero, I do not mean to represent him as above human weakness, and 1 won't pretend that he didn't feel anxious and disturbed. His prospects seemed very dark. He could not hope for mercy from the brutal men who had captured him. As they could not get hold of the giant they would undoubtedly seek to make him expiate the offenses of Achilles Henderson as well as his own.

"If only Mr. Henderson knew where I was," he said to himself, "I should soon be free."

But there seemed little hope of this. He had not told anyone that he intended to retire to the circus cars earlier than usual. The chances were that he would not be missed till the circus company had reached the next town on their route, ten miles away. Then there would be no clew to his whereabouts, and even if there were, he might be killed before any help could come to him. So far as he had been able to observe, the miners were—a portion of them, at least, —a lawless set of men, who were not likely to be influenced by considerations of pity or ordinary humanity.

Kit had been very religiously brought up during his father's life, at least, and he had not lost his faith in an overruling Providence. So in this great peril it was natural for him to pray to God for deliverance from danger. When his prayer was concluded, he felt easier, and in spite of his disagreeable surroundings he managed to fall asleep.

Meanwhile the circus performance terminated, and preparations were commenced for the journey to the next town. The canvas men swarmed around the tents and swiftly took them down and conveyed them to the freight cars, where they assisted the razorbacks to pack them in small compass.

Harry Thorne, who had his berth next to Kit, turned in rather late. He looked into Kit's bed, and to his surprise found it unoccupied.

"What can have become of the boy?" he asked himself.

He went outside, and espying Achilles Henderson, he said: "Have you seen anything of Kit Watson?"

"Isn't he in his berth?" asked Mr. Henderson, surprised.

" No."

Inquiry developed the fact that Kit had not been seen by anyone since the conclusion of his act.

" I am afraid the boy has come to harm," said Achilles. " This is a rough place, and there are plenty of tough characters about, as our experience this afternoon showed."

" What shall we do? The cars will soon be starting, and we must leave him behind."

" If he doesn't show up before that time, I will stay behind and hunt him up. He is too good a boy to be left to his fate."

CHAPTER XXVII.

A MINER'S CABIN.

Kit's principal captor was known as Dick Hayden. He was an Englishman, and a leader in every kind of mischief. If there was any disturbance between the miners and their employers, he was generally found to be at the bottom of it. A naturally quarrelsome disposition was intensified by intemperance. In the attack upon the circus tents he found himself in his element. His ignominious defeat made him ugly and revengeful.

His wife was dead, but he had one child, Janet, a girl of thirteen, who cooked for him and took care of his cabin. The poor girl had a hard time of it, but she endeavored so far as possible to avoid trouble with her brutal parent.

It was near ten o'clock when Hayden came home after locking Kit in the deserted cabin. He had gone away without supper, but late as it was, Janet had something hot ready for him on the stove.

" Well, Janet, child, have you my supper ready? " he said, not unpleasantly, for his victory over Kit and the meditated revenge of the next day had put him in good humor.

" Yes, father; it's on the stove and ready to dish up."

" Lay the table, then, for I'm main tired and hungry."

The little girl quickly spread the cloth, and Dick Hayden ate like a voracious animal.

When supper was over he sat back in his chair and lit a pipe. A comfortable supper made him loquacious.

" Well, Janet, you don't ask where I've been to-day."

" Was it to the circus, father? "

" Yes."

" How did you like the show? "

" I didn't see it," he growled, a frown gathering upon his brow.

"And why not, father?"

"Because we had to fight to get in free, and got the worst of it."

"They must be main strong, then, those circus men."

"Strong!" repeated Hayden, scornfully. "Well, mayhap they are, but we'd have bested them but for the giant."

"The giant! Is it the big man I saw in the parade?"

"Yes; he's as strong as three men. He flung me down as easily as I'd throw a boy."

"Then he must have been strong, for you're a powerful man, father."

"There isn't a man as works in the mine'll compare with me, lass," said Hayden, proudly; "but all the same I'm no match for a monster."

"Tell me about it, father," said Janet, with natural curiosity.

Dick Hayden went on to describe the fight around the ticket stand, and how he had slipped away, intending to cut the ropes of the tent and let it down on the heads of the spectators gathered inside.

"I'd have done it, too," he added, "but for the kid."

"I thought just now you said it was the giant."

"And I stuck to it, lass; but this boy saw what I was doing, and brought the giant to the spot. I could do nothing after that. He threw me down, so that for a few minutes I was stunned."

"And how did the fight come out at the ticket stand, father?"

"Our men had almost overpowered the circus men, when the giant rushed into the midst, and, seizing a club from Bob Stubbs, laid about him, till half a dozen of our strongest men lay on the ground with broken heads."

What puzzled Janet was, that her father should have come home in such good humor after so disastrous defeat. It was contrary to her experience of him. She would naturally have expected that he would be surly and quarrelsome. The mystery was soon made clear.

"But we've got even with them!" chuckled Hayden, directly after.

"How is that, father?"

"We caught the kid."

"You have?"

"Yes; he was goin' to the circus cars to turn in when Stubbs and I caught him."

"You—you didn't kill him, father?" asked Janet, in alarm.

"No, not yet."

"Where is he?"

"Do you mind the deserted cabin on Knob Hill?"

"Yes, father."

"He's locked up in that, tied hand and foot."

"How long do you mean to keep him there?" asked Janet, anxiously.

"Till to-morrow, and then—" Dick paused ominously.

"Well, and then?"

"He'll be lucky if he gets off with a whole skin," growled her father. "But for him I'd have brought down the tent about the ears of the people that sat inside, and we'd have had a fine revenge on the showmen."

"You don't mean to kill the boy, do you, father?"

"What is it to you, lass? You'd best mind your own business. You've got nothing to do with it."

"How does the boy look? Was it the one that drove the first chariot, father?"

"Like enough, lass! Did you see him?"

"Yes; I saw the parade. Everybody was out in the streets then."

"And you took partic'lar notice of the boy? That's like a lass," chuckled Hayden.

"But it was his duty, father, to stand by the show, seein' he belongs to it."

"I don't trouble myself about that. He brought that monster on me, and I'm sore yet with the fall he gave me. I'll take it out of the kid."

"But it seems to me, father, it would be better to lay for the giant."

"What folly is that, lass? I'd be main glad to give the giant a dose of what he gave me, but he'll leave town to-night, and I ain't big enough to tackle him, even if I had the chance. So I'll revenge myself on his friend, the boy. The kid may be his son, for aught I know."

"And what will you do to him, father?" asked Janet, pertinaciously. "You won't kill him?"

"Well, I won't go so far as that, for I've no mind to put my neck in a noose, but I'll flog him within an inch of his life. I'll teach him to mind his own business for the future."

Janet knew her father's strength and brutality, and she shuddered at the idea of the boy being exposed to it. She knew very well it would be of no use to make a protest. She would only get herself into trouble. Yet she couldn't reconcile herself to the thought of poor Kit being cruelly punished. She asked herself what she could do to prevent it.

There was one thing in favor of a rescue. She knew where Kit was confined. If it were not so late she would steal out, and going to the cabin relieve him from captivity. But it was too late, and too dark for that. Besides, she could not leave her father's cabin without observation.

"I will wait till to-morrow morning," she said to herself.

It so chanced that on account of some slight repairs the mine in which her father was employed was shut down for a few days. This was favorable, for he would lie in bed till eight o'clock at least, and there would be a chance to get out without observation.

The next morning, about five o'clock, Janet rose from her bed, hastily dressed herself, and crept to the door of her father's chamber. He was sound asleep, and breathing heavily. There was small chance of his awakening before seven o'clock.

Janet took a little meat and bread in a tin pail, for she thought the captive might be in need of breakfast, and then, putting a knife in her pocket to cut the ropes that bound him, she left the house and took her way over the hill to the deserted cabin which served as Kit's prison.

CHAPTER XXVIII.

KIT RESCUED BY A GIRL.

KIT had succeeded in getting a little sleep during the night, but his position was necessarily constrained and he was but very slightly refreshed. Moreover he was a prey to anxiety, for he did not know what fate awaited him on the succeeding day.

At four o'clock in the morning a little light found its way into the cabin through a small window at the rear. The other windows were boarded up.

Kit, appreciating the desirability of escaping before a visit should be made him by his captors, tried hard to work himself out of his bonds, but only succeeded in confining himself more closely than before.

"What will they do to me?" he asked himself, anxiously.

He had heard from some of the circus men accounts of the roughness and brutality of the miners, or at least of a certain class of them, for some were quiet and peaceable men, and he knew that there was no extreme of which they were not capable. Life is sweet, and to a boy of sixteen, in good health and strength, it is especially dear. Suppose he should lose his life in this region? Probably none of his friends would ever learn what had become of him, and his uncle and cousin would not scruple to spread rumors to his discredit.

It was certainly tantalizing that he should be tied hand and foot, utterly unable to help himself.

More and more light crept in at the window, and there was every indication of its being a glorious day. But this prospect brought no pleasure to poor Kit.

"Before this time the circus people must have found out

my absence," he thought. "Will they take the trouble to look for me?"

Kit was on good terms with his comrades, indeed he was popular with them all, as a bright boy is apt to be, and he did not like to think that no effort would be made to find him. Still, as he could not help owning to himself, they had no clew that was likely to lead to success. He had given no one notice where he was going, and his capture was not likely to have been observed by anyone.

While he was indulging in these sorrowful reflections, his attention was drawn to a noise at the window.

"They can't have come back so early," he said to himself, in surprise.

He twisted himself round to catch a glimpse, if possible, of the early visitor, and to his delight, he caught a partial view of Janet's dress. Suppose she should prove a deliverer, he said to himself with beating heart.

The visitor, whoever it was, was evidently trying to peer into the cabin. Kit was so placed in a corner as to be almost out of sight in the dark interior. He felt that he must attract attention.

"Hallo, there!" he cried in a loud clear voice.

"He's there!" thought Janet, "just as father said."

"Let me out!" cried Kit, eagerly. "Draw out the bolt, and open the door!"

"Will she do it, or will she be frightened away?" he asked himself, with his heart filled with suspense.

He did not have long to wait for an answer, and a favorable one. He heard the bolt withdrawn, then the door was opened, and the girl's face appeared. Janet Hayden was small, not especially pretty, and rather old-fashioned in looks, but to poor Kit she seemed like an angel.

"Are you the circus boy?" she asked, timidly.

"Yes; I am tied here. Have you got a knife to cut this rope?"

"Yes; I brought one with me."

"Then you knew I was here?" Kit asked, in surprise.

"Yes; it was my father that locked you up here—my father and another man."

"Will you cut the rope and let me go, then?"

"Yes; that is what I came for."

The little maid went up to the captive, bent over, and with considerable sawing, for the knife she had with her was a dull case knife, succeeded in severing the rope, and Kit was able to rise and stand upon his feet. It was a perfect luxury to feel himself once more free and unshackled.

"I'm very much obliged to you," he said, gratefully. "You can't imagine how stiff I am."

"I should think you would be," said Janet, sympathetically.

"When did your father tell you that I was here?"

"After he got home last night. It was after he had eaten his supper."

"And where is he now?"

"At home and asleep."

"Does he get up early?" asked Kit, in some anxiety.

"Yes, when he is at work; but the mine is shut down for a few days, so he lies abed longer."

"Did he say anything about coming here to-day?"

"Yes, he meant to come—he and the other man—and I was afraid that he would do you some harm."

"He would have done so, I am sure," said Kit, shuddering. "I don't see how such a rough father should have so good a daughter."

Janet blushed, and seemed pleased with the compliment.

"I think I take after my mother," she said.

"Is your mother alive?"

"No, she died two years ago," answered Janet, sorrowfully. "She was Scotch, and that is why I am called by a Scotch name."

"What is your name, if you don't mind telling me?"

"Janet. I am Janet Hayden."

"I shall always remember it, for you have done me a great service."

"What is your name?" asked Janet, feeling less timid than at first.

"Kit Watson."

"That is a funny name—Kit, I mean."

"My right name is Christopher, but my friends call me Kit. Can you direct me to the next town—Groveton, where the circus shows to-day?"

"Yes, if you will come outside, I will point out which way it is."

Kit emerged from the cabin, nothing loath, and Janet pointed in a westerly direction.

"You go over the hill," she said, "and you will come to a road. You will know it, for near the stile there is a red house."

"Thank you," said Kit. "How far is it to the next town?"

"Eight miles, I believe."

"That would be a long walk. Do you think I could get anyone to take me over in a wagon?"

"I think the man who lives in the red house, Mr. Stover, would take you over, if you pay him for it."

"I shall be glad to pay him, and—" Kit paused, for he felt rather delicate about offering any money to Janet, though he knew she had rendered him most valuable service. "Will you let me offer you a little present?"

He took a five-dollar bill from his pocket, and offered it to Janet.

"What is that?" she asked.

7 MM

"It is a five-dollar bill."

"You must be rich," she said, for this seemed to her a great deal of money.

"Oh, no! but will you take it?"

"No," answered Janet, shrinking back, "I didn't come here for money."

"I am sure you didn't, but I should like to give you something."

"No, I would rather not. Besides, if father knew I had money, he would suspect something, and beat me."

"Like the brute that he is," thought Kit.

"But I must go at once, for he may wake up and miss me. Good-by!"

"Good-by!" said Kit.

He had no time to say more, for the child was already hurrying down the hill.

CHAPTER XXIX.

JANET MEETS THE GIANT.

JANET took her way homeward, hurrying with quick feet, lest her father should wake up before she arrived. But she had taken so early a start that she found him still sleeping soundly. She instantly began to make preparations for breakfast.

By the time it was on the table her father woke up and yawned. With his waking there came the thought of his young circus captive, and the vengeance he intended to wreak upon him. This pleasant idea roused him completely, and he dressed himself briskly.

"Is breakfast ready, Janet?" he asked.

"Yes, father."

"What time is it?"

"Seven o'clock," answered Janet, looking at the clock over the mantel.

"I am expecting Bob Stubbs here this morning. Have you got enough for him?"

"I think so, father," replied Janet. She did not speak with alacrity, for Mr. Stubbs was no favorite of hers.

At that moment a step was heard at the door, and the gentleman spoken of made his appearance.

"You're late, Dick," said Stubbs, rubbing his bristling chin.

"Yes, I got tired out yesterday. When the mine's shut down I like to take my time. Have you had breakfast, Bob?"

"Ye-es," answered Stubbs, hesitating, as he glanced at

the neatly spread table, with the eggs and bacon on the center dish.

"Never mind! You can eat some more. Put a chair for him, Janet."

"This lass of yours is growing pretty," said Stubbs, with a glance of admiration.

"There's a compliment for you, lass!" said the father.

Janet, however, did not appear to appreciate it, and continued to look grave.

"Wonder how the kid's getting along," said Bob Stubbs, with his mouth full of bacon.

"I reckon he's hungry," said Dick Hayden, in a voice of satisfaction.

"Have you left him without anything to eat, father?" asked Janet.

"Yes."

"The poor fellow will be starved."

"And serves him right, too. There ain't no call to pity him."

"Why won't you take him some breakfast if you're going round there? I will put some up in a tin pail."

"What do you say to that, Bob, hey?" said Hayden.

"It's natural for the gal to pity him. He's a nice-lookin' chap enough."

"He's nicer looking than he will be when we get through with him; eh, Bob?"

"That's so, Dick."

As Janet listened to this conversation, her heart revolted against the brutality conveyed by the words. She felt dissatisfied to think that her own father was such a man. She could not well feel an affection for him, remembering how ill he had treated her gentle mother, who, as she knew, would be living to-day had she been wedded to a better husband.

The two men did not linger long at the table. They were accustomed to swallow their food rapidly, in order to get to the scene of their daily labor on time. So in twenty minutes they rose from the table, and putting on their hats left the cabin.

As they departed Janet breathed a sigh of relief, and congratulated herself that she had released the poor boy, and so saved him from the brutal treatment he was likely to receive at the hands of the two miners.

"He will have had plenty of time to get away before father and Mr. Stubbs reach the cabin," she said to herself.

Janet washed the dishes, and then, having an errand at the store, put on her hat and left the cabin. She did not trouble herself to lock the door, for there was nothing in the place likely to excite the cupidity of any dishonest person.

Janet had accomplished a part of the distance when she

saw approaching her a figure that at once attracted her earnest attention.

The reason will be readily understood when I say that it was Achilles Henderson, the circus giant.

Mr. Henderson had been exploring the neighborhood in the hope of finding some trace of Kit, but thus far had been unsuccessful. He was very much perplexed, having absolutely no clew, and was thinking of starting for Groveton, where the circus was billed to appear that evening. He was walking in an undecided way, and never thought of noticing the little girl who stood staring at him. Indeed he was so used to being stared at that he took it as a matter of course, and did not think of giving the curious gazer a second glance.

But his attention was called by a low, half-frightened voice.

"Mr. Giant!"

"Well, little girl, what do you want?" he asked.

"Are you looking for anybody?" asked Janet, first glancing carefully around, to make sure that she was not likely to be overheard.

"Yes," answered Achilles, quickly. "I am looking for a boy."

"A circus boy?"

"Yes; do you know where he is?"

"Come nearer! I don't want anybody to hear what I say."

"All right, my little maid! Is the boy alive and well?"

"Yes, he was two hours ago."

"Where is he?"

"I don't know where he is now."

Achilles looked disappointed.

"Tell me all you know," he said.

"My father and Bob Stubbs took him last night, and shut him up in a lonely cabin on the hill."

"Where is the cabin?"

"He isn't there now. I let him out."

"Good for you, little girl! You're a trump. You're a great deal better than your father. Do you know where the boy went?"

"I will tell you where I told him to go."

"Where is your father now? Is he at work?"

"No; the mine is shut down."

"How did you know that the boy was in the cabin?"

"I heard father tell where he was last night, when he was at supper. So I got up very early, and stole out to release him, for I was afraid father might kill him. He said he meant to punish him for what you did. He said he would rather get at you."

"He's quite welcome to, if he wants to," answered Achilles, grimly. "On the whole, I wouldn't advise him to tackle me."

" He thought you had gone on with the circus."

" I should have done so if I hadn't missed Kit."

" Yes; he told me his name was Kit."

" Was he tied? "

" Yes; I took a knife with me and cut the ropes."

" The poor fellow must have passed an uncomfortable night."

" Yes, he said so."

" He must have been very glad to see you."

" Yes, he was. I am only afraid of one thing."

" What is that? "

" Father and the other man left the house more than half an hour ago to go to the cabin. When they find him gone, they will be very angry."

" Like as not."

" And I think they will try to find him."

" Very true; I wish I knew where he was. They wouldn't dare to attack him in my company."

" No, Mr. Giant. You must be very strong."

" I think I would be a match for them."

Achilles questioned Janet minutely as to the advice she had given Kit.

" I might follow the boy," he said to himself, " at a guess, but there's only half a chance of my hitting right. Where is the cabin? ' he asked suddenly.

Janet pointed in the proper direction.

" I know what I'll do," he said, with sudden decision. " I'll follow your father and the other man. All the danger to Kit is likely to come from them. If I can get track of them, I can make sure that no mischief will be done."

Achilles Henderson then stepped over a fence which an ordinary man would have had to climb, and made his way to the deserted cabin.

CHAPTER XXX.

DICK HAYDEN FINDS THE BIRD FLOWN.

HALF an hour previously Dick Hayden and his congenial friend, Bob Stubbs, reached the cabin. They had much pleasant and jocose conversation on the way touching their young captive, and how he had probably passed the night. They had personal injuries to avenge, and though Achilles was responsible for them, they proposed to wreak vengeance on the boy whom a luckless fate had thrown into their hands.

" My shoulders are sore yet," said Hayden, " over the fall that big brute gave me."

"And my head hasn't got over the crock I got when he laid me flat with his club," responded Stubbs.

"Well, we've got a friend of his, that's one comfort. I'm going to take it out of the kid's hide."

"You don't mean to—do for him?" said Stubbs, cautiously.

"I don't mean to kill him, if that's what you mean, Stubbs. I have too much regard for my neck, but I mean to give him a sound flogging. You ain't afraid, be you?"

"Catch Bob Stubbs afraid of anything except the hangman's rope! I don't mind telling you that I have reasons to be afraid of that."

"Why? You've never been hung, have you?"

"No; but an uncle of mine was strung up in England."

"What for?"

"He got into trouble with a fellow workman and stabbed him."

"He was in bad luck. Why didn't he cut it, and come to America?"

"He tried it, but the bobbies caught him in the steerage of an ocean steamer, and then it was all up with him."

"Well, I hope his nephew will come to a better end. But here we are at the cabin."

There was nothing in the outward appearance of the hut to indicate that the bird was flown. Janet bolted the door after releasing the prisoner, and no one could judge that it had been opened.

"All is safe," said Bob Stubbs.

"Of course it is! Why shouldn't it be?"

"No reason; but some of his friends might have found him."

"All his friends are at Groveton. Then they had no idea what we did with him."

"They must have found out that he was gone."

"They couldn't find him, so that would do him no good."

Stubbs was about to draw the bolt, but Hayden stayed his hand.

"Wait a minute, Bob," he said; "I'll look in at the window, and see what he is doing."

Dick Hayden went around to the rear of the building, and flattened his face against the pane in the effort to see the corner where the captive had been tied. He could not see very distinctly, but what he did see startled him.

He could perceive no one.

"Could the boy have loosened the rope?" he asked himself, hurriedly.

Even in that case, as the window was nailed so that it could not be opened, and the door was bolted, there seemed no way of escape. His eyes eagerly explored other portions of the cabin, but he could not catch a glimpse of Kit.

He rushed round to the front, and in an excitement which Stubbs could not understand, pulled the bolt back with a jerk.

"What's the matter, Dick?" asked Stubbs, staring.

Dick Hayden did not answer, but threw open the door.

He strode in, and peeped here and there.

"The boy is gone!" he said, hoarsely, to Stubbs, who followed close behind.

"Gone!" echoed Stubbs, in blank amazement. "How did he get away?"

"That's the question," responded Dick, growling.

"Well, I'm flabbergasted! There's witchery here!"

Dick Hayden bent over and picked up the pieces of rope which lay in the corner where the prisoner had been placed. He examined the ends, and said briefly, turning to Stubbs: "They've been cut!"

"So they have, Dick. Who in natur' could have done it? Perhaps the kid did it himself. Might have had a knife in his pocket."

"Don't be a fool, Stubbs! Supposin' he'd done it, how was he goin' to get out?"

"That's what beats me!"

"Somebody must have let him out."

"Do you think it's his circus friends?"

"No; they're all in Groveton. Somebody must have been passin' and heard the boy holler, and let him out."

"What are you goin' to do about it, Dick?"

"Goin' to sit down and take a smoke. It may give me an idea."

It will be noticed that of these two, Dick Hayden, as the bolder and stronger spirit, was the leader, and Bob Stubbs the subservient follower. Stubbs was no less brutal, when occasion served, but he was not self-reliant. He wanted someone to lead the way, and he was willing to follow.

The two men sat down beside the cabin, and lit their pipes. Nothing was said for a time. Dick seemed disinclined to conversation, and Stubbs was always disposed to be silent when enjoying a smoke.

The smoke continued for twenty minutes or more.

Finally Dick withdrew the pipe from his mouth.

"Well, Dick, what do you think about it? What shall we do?" inquired his friend.

"I am going to foller the kid."

"But you don't know where he's gone," replied Stubbs.

"No; but I may strike his track. Are you with me?"

"Of course I am."

"Then listen to me. The one that let the boy out knows the neighborhood. The boy would naturally want to go to Groveton, and likely he would be directed to Stover. If the kid had any money, he would ask Stover to drive him over, or else he would foot it."

" You're right, Dick. That's what he'd do," said Stubbs,
admiring his companion's penetration.

" Then we must go over to Stover's."

" All right! I'm with you."

" I'm a poor man, Bob, but I'd give a ten-dollar bill to
have that kid in my power once more."

" I don't doubt it, Dick."

" I hate to have it said that a kid like that got the advantage of Dick Hayden."

" So would I, Dick."

" If I get hold of him I'll give him a lesson that he won't
soon forget."

" And serve him right, too."

The two men rose and took their way across the fields,
following exactly the same path which our hero had traveled earlier in the morning.

They walked with brisk steps, having a definite purpose
in view. Dick Hayden was intensely anxious to recapture
Kit, whose escape had balked him of his vengeance, and
mortified him exceedingly. As he expressed it, he could
not bear to think that a boy of sixteen had got the advantage of him.

At length they reached the red house already referred to,
and saw Ham Stover, the owner, in the yard.

" You are up betimes, Dick," said Stover. " What's in
the wind? "

" Have you seen aught of a boy of sixteen passin' this
way? " asked Dick, anxiously.

" A likely-lookin' lad, well dressed? "

" Yes."

" He was round here an hour ago, and took breakfast in
the house."

This was true; the slight refreshment Janet had brought
him having proved insufficient to completely stay the crav-
ings of Kit's appetite after his night in the cabin.

" Where is he now? "

" What do you want of him? "

" Never you mind—I'll tell you bimeby. Where is he? "

" He wanted me to harness up and take him to Groveton."

Dick Hayden and Stubbs exchanged glances. It was evident that they had struck Kit's trail.

" Well, did you do it? "

" No; I couldn't spare the time. Besides I wanted the
horse to go to the village. I'm going to harness up now."

" What did the boy do? "

" He walked."

" How long since did he start? "

" About half an hour or thereabouts."

Dick Hayden made a rapid calculation.

"We may overtake him if we walk fast," he said.
Without stopping to enlighten the curiosity of Mr. Stover,
the two men set out rapidly on the Groveton road.

CHAPTER XXXI.

IN THE ENEMY'S HANDS.

Mr. Stover was considerably surprised when twenty minutes later, looking up from his work in the yard, he saw a
man of colossal size crossing the street. He hadn't attended
the circus, and had not therefore heard of the giant, who
was one of its principal features.

"Who in creation can that be?" Stover asked himself.

Achilles Henderson turned into the yard and accosted the
farmer.

"Good-morning, friend," he said. "Can you tell me if
a boy of about sixteen has passed here this morning?"

"That boy again!" thought the bewildered farmer.

"Yes," he answered.

"Please describe him."

Mr. Stover did so.

"The very one!" said Achilles. "Now how long since
was he here?"

"He took breakfast with my family, and started off nigh
on to an hour ago."

"In what direction did he go?"

This question was also answered.

"Thank you, friend," said the giant; "you have done me
a favor."

"Then won't you do me one?" said Stover. "Who is this
boy that so many people are askin' for?"

"He is a young acrobat connected with Barlow's circus.
But what do you mean by so many people asking about
him?"

"There was two men here twenty minutes ago, that
seemed very anxious to find him."

Achilles Henderson heard this with apprehension. He
could guess who they were, and what he heard alarmed him
for Kit's safety.

"Who are they?" he inquired, hastily.

"Dick Hayden and Bob Stubbs."

"Are they miners?"

"Yes."

"Did you tell them where the boy went?"

"Sartin! Why not?"

"Because they mean to do the boy a mischief; they may
even kill him."

"What in creation should they do that for?"

"Mr. Stover, I must follow them at once. Have you a team?"

"Yes; but I calculated to use it."

"I must have it, and I want you to go with me. You may charge what you please. Remember a boy's life may depend on it."

"Then you shall have it," said the farmer, "and I'll go with you. I took a likin' to the boy. He was a gentleman, if ever I saw one; and my women folks was mightily taken with him. Dick Hayden and Bob Stubbs are rough kind of men, and I wouldn't trust anyone I set store by in their hands. But why——"

"Harness your horse, and I'll answer your questions on the way, Mr. Stover."

"How do you know my name?" asked Stover, with sudden thought.

"I was told by someone as I came along."

The farmer lost no time in harnessing his horse, Achilles Henderson lending a hand. The horse seemed rather alarmed, never having seen a giant before, but soon got over his fright. The two men then jumped into the wagon, and set out in search of Kit.

Meanwhile our hero had taken his way leisurely along the road. He didn't anticipate being followed, at any rate so soon, and felt under no particular apprehension. He had walked about three miles when a broad, branching elm tree tempted him to rest by its shade. He threw himself down on the grass, and indulged in self-congratulations upon his escape from his captors. But his congratulation proved to be premature. After a while he raised his eyes and looked carelessly back in the direction from which he had come. What he saw startled him.

The two miners, Hayden and Stubbs, had lost no time on the way. They were bent on capturing Kit, in order to revenge themselves upon him.

Reaching a little eminence in the road, Dick Hayden caught sight of his intended victim sitting under the tree.

His eyes gleamed with a wicked light.

"There's the kid, Stubbs!" he said. "Stir your stumps, old man, and we'll collar him!"

The two miners started on a run, and when Kit caught sight of them they were already within a few rods. The young acrobat saw that his only safety, if indeed there was any chance at all, was in flight. He started to his feet, and being fleet of limb gave them a good chase. But in the end the superior strength and endurance of the men conquered. Flushed and panting, Kit was compelled to stop. Hayden grasped him by the collar with a look of wicked satisfaction.

"So I've got you, my fine chap, have I?"

" Yes, so it seems! " said Kit, with a sinking heart.

" Sit down! I've got a few questions to ask."

There was a broad, flat stone by the roadside. He seated Kit upon it with a forcible push, and the two men ranged themselves one on each side of him.

" What time did you leave the cabin, boy? "

" I don't know what time it was. It must have been two hours since—perhaps more."

" Did anyone let you out? "

" Yes."

" Who was it? "

" I don't know the person's name."

" Was it a man? "

Kit began to feel that he must be cautious. He knew that she was the daughter of the man who was questioning him, and that she would be in danger of rough treatment if her father should find out that she had thwarted him.

" I cannot tell you," he answered, though he well knew that the answer was likely to get him into trouble.

" You can't tell? Why not? Don't you know whether it was a man or not? "

" Yes, I know."

" You mean that you won't tell me, then? " said Hayden, in a menacing tone.

" I mean that I don't care to do it. I might get the person into trouble."

" You would that, you may bet your life. I can tackle any man round here, and I'd get even with that man if I swung for it."

" That is why I don't care to tell you," said Kit. " How can you tell that the man knew you put me there? "

" Didn't you tell him? "

" No."

" It was a man, then! " said Hayden, turning to Stubbs. " Look here, young feller, if you tell me who it was, you may get off better yourself."

" I would rather not! " answered Kit, pale but firm.

" Suit yourself, kid, but you may as well know that you'll be half killed before we get through with you. Get up! "

As he spoke, Hayden jerked Kit to his feet, and began to drag him toward the rail fence.

" Take down the rails, Stubbs! " he said.

" What's your game, Dick? "

" I'm going to give the kid a drubbing that he won't be likely to forget, but I can't do it in the road, for someone may come along."

" I'm with you, Dick."

At the lower end of the field which they had now entered was a strip of woods, which promised seclusion and freedom

from interruption. Poor Kit, as he was dragged forward by
his relentless captor, found his spirits sinking to zero.
"Will no one deliver me from this brutal man?" he exclaimed, inwardly.

He felt that his life was in peril.

CHAPTER XXXII.

KIT'S DANGER.

THE men reached the edge of the woods and halted.

"I'd like to hang him!" growled Dick Hayden, with a
malignant look.

"It wouldn't do, Dick," said Stubbs. "We'd get into
trouble."

"If we were found out."

"Murder will 'most always come out," said Stubbs, uneasily. He was a shade less brutal and far less daring than
his companion.

It can be imagined with what feelings Kit heard this col-
loquy. He had no confidence in the humanity of his captors,
and considered them, Dick Hayden in particular, as capable
of anything. He did not dare to remonstrate lest in a spirit
of perversity the two men might proceed to extremities.

Kit was not long in doubt as to the intentions of his
captors.

"Take off your coat, boy!" said Hayden, harshly.

Kit looked into the face of his persecutor, and decided
that it would be prudent to obey. Otherwise he would have
forcibly resisted.

He removed his coat and held it over his arm.

"Lay down the coat and take off your vest," was the next
order.

This also Kit felt compelled to do.

Dick Hayden produced from the capacious side-pocket of
his coat a cord, which he proceeded to test by pulling. It
was evidently very strong.

"Stubbs, tie him to yonder sapling!" said Dick.

Stubbs proceeded, nothing loath, to obey the directions of
his leader. Kit was tied with his back exposed. Dick Hayden watched the preparations with evident enjoyment.

"This is the moment I have been longing for," he said.

From the other pocket he drew a cowhide, which he passed
through the fingers of his left hand, while with cruel eyes
he surveyed the shrinking form of his victim.

Meanwhile where was Achilles Henderson?

He and Stover bowled as rapidly over the road as the

speed of a fourteen-year-old horse would permit. He looked eagerly before him, in the hope of catching a glimpse either of Kit or of the miners. When they started they were far behind, but at last they reached a point on the road where they could see Kit and his captors making their way across the fields.

"There they are!" said Stover, who was the first to see them.

"And they've got the boy with them!" ejaculated Achilles.

"Where are they going, do you think?"

"Over to them woods, it's likely," replied Stover.

"What for?"

"I'm afraid they mean to do the boy harm."

"Not if I can prevent it," said Achilles, with a stern look about the mouth.

"They're goin' to give him a floggin', I think."

"They'll get the same dose in larger measure, I can tell them that. Mr. Stover, isn't there any way I can reach the woods by a short cut so that they won't see me?"

"Yes, there is a path in that field there. There is a fringe of trees separatin' it from the field where they are walkin'."

"Then stop your horse, and I'll jump out!"

Mr. Stover did so with alacrity. He disliked both Dick Hayden and Bob Stubbs, whom he had reason to suspect of carrying off a dozen of his chickens the previous season. He had not dared to charge them with it, knowing the men's ugly disposition, and being certain that they would revenge themselves upon him.

"Do you want me along, Mr. Giant?" he asked.

"No; I'm more than a match for them both."

"Shouldn't wonder if you were," chuckled Stover.

He kept his place in the wagon and laughed quietly to himself.

"I'd like to see the scrimmage," he said to himself.

With this object in view he drove forward, so that from the wagon seat he could command a view of the scene of conflict.

"They're tying the boy to a tree," he said. "I reckon the giant'll be in time, and I'm glad on't. That boy's a real gentleman. Wonder what he's done to rile Dick Hayden and Bob Stubbs. He'd have a mighty small show if the giant hadn't come up. Dick's a strong man, but he'll be like a child in the hands of an eight-footer."

Meanwhile Achilles Henderson was getting over the ground at the rate of ten miles an hour or more. His long strides gave him a great advantage over an ordinary runner.

"If they lay a hand on that boy I pity 'em!" he said to himself.

It was fortunate for Kit that Dick Hayden, like a cat who plays with a mouse, paused to gloat over the evident alarm and uneasiness of his victim, even after all was ready for the punishment which he proposed to inflict.

"Well boy, what have you to say now?" he demanded, drawing the cowhide through his short, stubby fingers.

"I have nothing to say that will move you from your purpose, I am afraid," replied poor Kit.

"I guess you're about right there, kid!" chuckled Hayden. "Are you ready to apologize to me for what you done over to the circus?"

"I don't think there is anything to apologize for."

"There isn't, isn't there? Didn't you bring that long-legged ruffian on to me?"

"I was only doing my duty," said Kit, manfully.

"Oho! so that's the way you look at it, do you?"

"Yes, sir."

"No doubt you'd like it if that tall brute were here now," said Hayden, tauntingly.

"Yes," murmured Kit; "I wish my good friend Achilles were here."

"So that's his name, is it? Well, I wouldn't mind if he were here. Stubbs, I think you and I could do for him, eh?"

"I don't know," said Stubbs, dubiously.

"Well, I do. He's only one man, while we are two, and strong at that."

"Oho!" thought Achilles, who was now within hearing. "So my friend, the miner, is getting valorous! Well, he will probably have a chance to test his strength."

By this time Hayden had got through with his taunts, and was ready to enjoy his vengeance.

"Your time has come, boy!" he said, fiercely. "Stand back, Stubbs!"

Bob Stubbs stepped back, and Dick Hayden raised the cruel cowhide in his muscular grasp. It would have inflicted a terrible blow had it fallen on the young acrobat. But something unexpected happened. The instrument of torture was torn from his hands, and a deep voice, which he knew only too well, uttered these words: "For shame, you brute! Would you kill the boy?"

Panic-stricken, the brutal miner turned and found himself confronting Achilles Henderson.

A fierce cry of rage and disappointment burst from his lips.

"Where did you come from?" he stammered.

"From Heaven, I think!" murmured poor Kit, with devout gratitude to that overruling Providence which had sent him such a helper in his utmost need.

CHAPTER XXXIII.

DICK HAYDEN MEETS WITH RETRIBUTION.

DICK HAYDEN and Bob Stubbs, large and strong men as they were, looked puny, compared with the giant who towered beside them, his face kindling with righteous indignation.

"What were you going to do to the boy?" he demanded, sternly.

"I was going to flog him," answered Hayden, in a surly tone.

"And you were helping him?" went on Achilles, turning to Stubbs.

"No, sir," answered Stubbs, eagerly, for, big as he was, he was a coward. "I didn't want Dick to do it."

"You coward!" exclaimed Hayden, contemptuously. "You're as deep in it as I am."

"Is that true, Kit?" asked Achilles.

"He isn't as bad as the other," said Kit. "That man Hayden thought of killing me, but his friend protested against it."

"It shall be remembered to his credit. Why did you wish to flog the boy?" he asked of Hayden.

"On account of what happened at the circus."

"The boy didn't touch you."

"He brought you on me."

"Then I was the one to punish."

"I couldn't get at you."

"Here I am at your service."

Dick Hayden measured the giant with a vindictive eye, but there was something in the sight of the mighty thews and sinews of the huge man that quelled his warlike ardor.

"It wouldn't be a fair contest," he said, sullenly.

"There are two of you, as you said just before I came."

"No, there are not," interposed Stubbs, hastily. "I hain't any grudge against you, Mr. Giant."

"You are willing to help me?"

"Yes."

"Then untie that boy."

Stubbs unloosed the cord that bound Kit to the tree, while Achilles Henderson watched Hayden narrowly, for he had no mind to let him go free.

"Are you that man's slave?" asked Hayden.

"I am willing to oblige him," said Stubbs, meekly.

Kit straightened up on being released, and breathed a sigh of relief.

"Come along, Stubbs," said Hayden, with an ugly look at Kit and his protector. "Our business is through."

"Not quite," said Achilles, quietly, as he laid his broad hand with a detaining grasp on the shoulder of the ruffian. "I am not through with you."

"What do you want?" asked Dick Hayden, with assumed bravado, but with an uneasy look on his lowering face.

"I am going to give you a lesson. I gave you one at the circus ground, but you need another."

"Touch me if you dare!" said Hayden, defiantly.

For answer, Achilles hurled him to the ground with less effort than Hayden would have needed to serve Kit in the same way. Then with the cowhide uplifted he struck the prostrate wretch three sharp blows that made him howl with rage and pain. Stubbs looked on with pale face, thinking that his turn might come next.

"Hit him, Stubbs! Kill him!" screamed Dick Hayden. "Would you stand by and see me murdered?"

"I can't help you," said Stubbs. "What can I do?"

Having administered justice to the chief ruffian, Achilles turned to Stubbs.

"Now," he said, "what have you to say for yourself? Why shouldn't I serve you in the same way?"

"Spare me!" whined Stubbs, panic-stricken. "I am the boy's friend. It was Hayden who wanted to hurt him."

"My friend, I put very little confidence in what you say. Still I don't think you are as bad as this brute here. I will spare you on one condition."

"What is it? Indeed, I will do anything you ask."

"Then take this cowhide and give your companion a taste of its quality."

Stubbs looked alarmed.

"Don't ask me to do that," he said. "Me and Dick are pals."

"Just as I supposed. In that case you require a dose of the same medicine," and Achilles made a threatening demonstration with the rawhide.

"Don't do it," cried Stubbs, affrighted.

"Then will you do as I say?"

"Yes, yes."

"Will you lay it on well?"

"Yes," answered Stubbs, who, forced to choose between his own skin and Hayden's, was influenced by a regard for his own person.

Dick Hayden listened to this conference with lowering brow. He did not think Stubbs would dare to hit him. But he was destined to find himself unpleasantly surprised.

Stubbs took the hide from the hands of the giant, and anxious to conciliate his powerful antagonist laid it with emphasis on Hayden, already smarting from his former castigation.

"I'll kill you for that, Bob Stubbs!" he yelled, almost frothing at the mouth with rage.

"I had to do it Dick!" said Stubbs, apologetically. "You heard what he said."

"I don't care what he said. To spare your own miserable carcass, you struck your friend. But I am your friend no longer. I'll have it out of you!"

"Come, Kit, you are revenged," said the giant. "Now let us hurry on to the circus. There's a team in the road below. I think I can make a bargain with Mr. Stover to carry us all the way."

They found Mr. Stover waiting for them.

"Well," he said, "how did you make out?"

"Suppose you look back and see!"

Stover did look, and to his amazement he saw Dick Hayden and Bob Stubbs rolling on the ground, each holding the other in a fierce embrace. Hayden had attacked Stubbs, and though the latter tried hard to avoid a combat he was forced into it. Then, finding himself pushed, he fought as well as he could. Fortune favored him, for Dick Hayden tripped, and in so doing sprained his ankle. He fell with a groan, and Stubbs, glad to escape, left him in haste, and made the best of his way home.

It was not until several hours afterwards that Hayden was found by another party, and carried home, where he was confined for a fortnight. This was fortunate for Kit and the giant, for he had intended to make a formal complaint before a justice of the peace which might have resulted in the arrest and detention of one or both. But his sprained ankle gave him so much pain that it drove all other thoughts out of his head for the time being.

Mr. Stover was induced by an unusually liberal offer to convey the two friends to the next town, where thy found their circus friends wondering what had become of them. Kit was none the worse for his experience, though it had been far from pleasant, and performed that afternoon and evening with his usual spirit and success.

He told Achilles how he had been rescued by Janet Hayden, and the latter said with emphasis: "The girl's a trump! She has probably saved your life! That brute, her father, wouldn't shrink from any violence, no matter how great. You ought to make her some acknowledgment, Kit."

"I wouldn't dare to," answered the young acrobat. "If her father should find out what she did for me, I am afraid her life would not be safe."

CHAPTER XXXIV.

SOME IMPORTANT INFORMATION.

Two or three days later, the circus was billed to show at Glendale, a manufacturing village in Western Pennsylvania. The name attracted the attention of Kit, for this was the place where his uncle had lived for many years previous to the death of Kit's father. He naturally desired to learn something of his uncle's reputation among the villagers, who, from his long residence among them, must remember him well.

The circus had arrived during the night. As a general thing Kit was not in a hurry to get up, but as he was to stay but a day in Glendale, he rose early, with the intention of improving his time.

Breakfast in the circus tent was not ready till nine o'clock, for circus men of every description get up late, except the razorbacks, who are compelled to be about very early to unload the freight cars, and the canvas men, who put up the tents. So Kit went to the hotel, and, registering his name, called for breakfast.

After he had eaten it, he strolled into the office, hoping to meet someone of whom he could make inquiries respecting his uncle. This was made unexpectedly easy. A man of about his uncle's age had been examining the list of arrivals. He looked at Kit inquisitively.

"I beg your pardon, young man," he said, "but are you Christopher Watson?"

"Yes, sir," answered Kit, politely.

"Did you ever have any relatives living in this place?"

"Yes, sir. My uncle, Stephen Watson, used to live here."

"I thought so. I once saw your father. He came here to visit your uncle. You look like him."

Kit was gratified, for he cherished a warm affection for his dead father, and was glad to have it said that he resembled him.

"Are you going to stay here long?" asked the villager.

"No, sir; I am here only for the day."

"On business, I presume."

"Yes, sir," answered Kit, smiling. "I am here with Barlow's circus."

The other looked amazed.

"You don't mean to say that you are connected with the circus?" he exclaimed.

"Yes, sir."

"In what capacity?"

"I am an acrobat."

"I don't understand it at all. Why should your father's son need to travel with a circus?"

"Because I have my living to earn, and that pays me better than any other employment I can get."

"But your father was a rich man, I always heard."

"I supposed so myself, till a short time since my uncle informed me that I was penniless, and must learn a trade."

"But where did the money go, then? How does your uncle make a living?"

"He has my father's old place, and appears to have enough to support himself and Ralph."

"Sit down here, young man! There is something strange about this. I want to ask you a few questions."

"You are the man I want to see," said Kit. "I think myself there is some mystery, and I would like to ask some questions about my Uncle Stephen from someone who knew him here. I suppose you knew him?"

"No one knew him better. Many is the time he has come to me for a loan. He didn't always pay back the money, and I dare say he owes me still in the neighborhood of fifty dollars."

"Was he poor then?"

"He was in very limited circumstances. He pretended to be in the insurance business, and had a small office in the building near the hotel, but if he made four hundred dollars a year in that way it was more than anyone supposed."

"Then," said Kit, puzzled, "how could he have lent my father ten thousand dollars?"

"He lend your father ten thousand dollars, or anybody else ten thousand dollars! Why, that is perfectly ridiculous. Who says he did?"

"He says so himself."

"To whom did he tell that fish story?"

"He told me. That is the way he explained his taking possession of the property. That was only one loan. He said he lent father money at various times, and had to take the estate in payment."

Kit's auditor gave a loud whistle.

"The man's a deeper and shrewder rascal than I had any idea of," he said. "He is swindling you in the most barefaced manner."

"I am not very much surprised to hear it," said Kit. "I was not satisfied that he was telling the truth. If you are correct, then he has wrongfully appropriated my father's money."

"There is no doubt on it. Did he drive you from home?"

"About the same. He attempted to apprentice me to a blacksmith, while his own son Ralph he means to send to college, and have him study law."

"I remember Ralph well, though he was a small boy when he left this village. He was very unpopular among those of his own age. He was always up to some mean act of mischief. He got my boy into trouble once in school by charging him with something he had himself done."

"He hasn't changed much, then," said Kit. "We both attended the same boarding school, but nobody liked Ralph."

"Was he much of a scholar?"

"No; he dragged along in the lower half of the class."

"Were you two good friends?"

"We didn't quarrel, but we kept apart."

"So his father wants to make a lawyer of him?"

"Yes; I have had a letter from Smyrna in which I hear that my uncle has just bought Ralph a bicycle valued at a hundred and twenty-five dollars."

"Money seems to be more plenty with him now than it used to be in his Glendale days. By the way, would you like to see the place where your uncle used to live?"

"Yes, sir, if you don't mind showing me."

"I will do so with pleasure. Put on your hat, and we will go at once."

They walked about a third of a mile, till they reached the outskirts of the village.

"This is the home of the foreign population," said Kit's guide. "And there is the house which was occupied for at least ten years by your uncle."

Kit eyed the building with interest. It was a plain-looking cottage, containing but four rooms, which stood badly in need of paint. There was about an acre of land, rocky and sterile, attached to it.

"This is the residence of the man who lent your father ten thousand dollars," said his guide, in an ironical tone. "Not much of a palace, is it?"

"It can't be worth over a thousand dollars."

"Your uncle sold it for seven hundred and eighty dollars, but he didn't get that sum in money, for it was mortgaged for six hundred."

"You say my father came here once?"

"It was to visit your uncle. While he was here, he stood security at the tailor's for new suits for your uncle and cousin, and must have given your uncle some cash besides, for he appeared to be in funds for some time afterwards. So you see the loan, or rather gift, was on the other side."

"I don't see how my uncle dared to misrepresent matters in that way."

"Nor I; for he could easily be convicted of fraudulent statements."

"I am very much obliged to you, Mr.——"

"Pierce."

"Mr. Pierce, for your information."

" I hope you will make some use of it."

" I certainly shall," said Kit, his good-humored face show-ing unwonted resolution.

" Whenever you do, my testimony will be at your service, and there are plenty others who will corroborate my state-ments of your uncle's financial condition when here. The fact is, my young friend, your uncle has engaged in a most shameless plot against you."

Kit was deeply impressed by this conversation. He was resolved, when the time came, to assert his rights, and lay, claim to his dead father's property.

CHAPTER XXXV.

ON THE TRAPEZE.

KIT was on pleasant relations with his fellow performers. Indeed, he was a general favorite, owing to his obliging dis-position and pleasant manners. He took an interest in their acts as well as his own, and in particular had cultivated an intimacy with Louise Lefroy, the trapeze performer. He had practiced on the trapeze in the gymnasium, and had acquired additional skill under the tuition of Mlle. Lefroy.

" Some time you will make an engagement as a trapeze performer, Christopher," said the lady to him one day.

" No," answered Kit, shaking his head.

" You wouldn't be afraid? "

" No; I think I would make a very respectable performer; but I don't mean to travel with the circus after this season, unless I am obliged to."

" Why should you be obliged to? "

" Because I have my living to earn."

" It is a pity," said Mlle. Lefroy. " You seem cut out for a circus performer."

" Do you like it, Mlle. Lefroy? "

The lady looked thoughtful.

" I have to like it," she said. " Besides, there is an excite-ment about it, and I crave excitement."

" But wouldn't you rather have a home of your own? "

" Listen! I had a home of my own, but my husband was intemperate, and in fits of intoxication would ill-treat me and my boy."

" Then you have a boy? " said Kit, surprised.

" Yes; and I support him at a boarding school out of my professional earnings, which are large."

"I am going to ask you another question, but you may not like to answer it."

"Speak plainly."

"Your husband is living, is he not?"

"Yes."

"Does he know that you are a circus performer?"

"No; I would not have him know for worlds."

"Would he feel sensitive about it?"

Mlle. Lefroy laughed bitterly.

"You don't know him, or you would not ask that question," she said. "He would want to appropriate my salary. That is why I do not care to have him know how I am earning the living which he ought to provide for me."

"I sympathize with you," said Kit, gently.

"Then you don't think any the worse of me because I am a trapeze performer?"

"Why should I? Am I not a circus performer also?"

"Yes; but it is different with you, being a man. You would not like to think of your mother or sister in my position."

"No; I would not, yet I can imagine circumstances that would justify it."

From this time Kit was disposed to look with different eyes upon Mlle. Lefroy. He did not think of her as a daring actor, but rather as an injured wife and devoted mother, who every day risked her life for the sake of one who was dear to her.

"Did you never fear that your husband might be present when you are performing?" asked Kit.

"It is my constant dread," answered Mlle. Lefroy. "When I come out in my costume, and look over the sea of heads, I am always afraid I shall see *his* face."

"But you never have yet?"

"Never yet. I do not think, if I should see that man, I would go through my part. It requires nerve, as you know, and my nerves would be so shaken that my life would be in peril. If you ever hear of my meeting with an accident, you may guess the probable cause."

"Then, if ever you recognize your husband among the spectators, it would be prudent to omit your performance."

"That is what I propose to do."

Kit little imagined how soon the contingency which his friend feared would arrive.

Two evenings later Harry Thorne brought him a little note. He opened it and read as follows:

"Come and see me at once.   LOUISE LEFROY."

Kit ascertained where Mlle. Lefroy was to be found, and obeyed the summons immediately.

He found the lady in great agitation.

"Are you not well?" he asked.

"Well in health, but not in mind," she answered.

"Has anything happened?"

"Yes; what I dreaded has come to pass."

"Have you seen your husband?" asked Kit, quickly.

"Yes; I was taking a walk, and saw him on the opposite side of the street."

"Did he see you?"

"No; but I ascertained that he is staying at the hotel. Now he is likely to follow the crowd, and attend the circus to-night."

"That is probable. Then you will not appear."

"I should not dare to. But it will be a great disappointment to the management. The trapeze act is always a popular one, especially in a country town like this. Now I am going to ask a favor of you."

Kit's face flushed with excitement. He foresaw what it would be.

"What is it?" he asked.

"I want you to appear in my place this evening."

"Do you think I am competent?"

"You cannot do my act, but you can do enough to satisfy the public. But, my dear friend, I don't want to subject you to any risk. If you are at all nervous or afraid, don't attempt it."

"I am not afraid," said Kit, confidently. "I will appear!"

In the evening the tent was full. Very few knew of the change in the programme. Mr. Barlow had consented to the substitution with some reluctance, for he feared that Kit might be undertaking something beyond his power to perform. Even the Vincenti brothers, Kit's associates, were surprised when the manager came forward and said:

"Ladies and gentlemen, Mlle. Lefroy is indisposed, and will be unable to perform her act this evening. Unwilling to disappoint the public, we have substituted one of our youngest and most daring performers, who will appear in her place."

When Kit came out, his young face glowing with excitement, and made his bow, the crowd of spectators greeted him with enthusiastic applause. His fellow actors joined in the ovation. They feared he had overrated his ability, but were ready to applaud his pluck.

Now was the time, if ever, for Kit to grow nervous, and show stage fright. But he felt none. The sight of the eager faces around him only stimulated him. He caught the rope which hung down from the trapeze, and quickly climbing up, poised himself on his elevated perch.

He did not allow himself to look down, but strove to shut out the sight of the hundreds of upturned faces, and pro-

ceeded to perform his act as coolly as if he were in a gymnasium, only six feet from the ground instead of thirty.

It is not to be supposed that Kit, who was a comparative
novice, could equal Mlle. Louise Lefroy, who had been cul-
tivating her specialty for ten years. He went through several feats, however, hanging from the trapeze with his head
down, then quickly recovering himself and swinging by his
hands. The public was disposed to be pleased, and, when
the act was finished, gave him a round of applause.

Later in the evening a small man, with a very dark complexion, and keen, black eyes, approached him as he was
standing near the lion's cage.

"Is this Luigi Vincenti?" he asked.

This was Kit's circus name. He passed for a brother of
Alonzo and Antonio Vincenti.

"Yes, sir," answered Kit.

"I saw your trapeze act this evening," he went on. "It
was very good."

"Thank you, sir. You know, perhaps, that I am not a
trapeze performer. I only appeared in place of Mlle. Lefroy,
who is indisposed."

"So I understand; but you do very well for a boy. My
name is Signor Oponto. I am at the head of a large circus
in Havana. My visit to the United States is partly to secure
additional talent. How long are you engaged to Mr. Barlow?"

"For no definite time. I suppose I shall remain till the
end of the season."

"You have no engagements beyond?"

"No, sir; this is my first season with any circus."

"Then I will make you an offer. I don't want to take you
from Mr. Barlow, but when the season is over I shall be
ready to arrange for your appearance in Havana under my
personal management."

Though Kit was modest he was human. He did feel flat-
tered to find himself rated so high. It even occurred to him
that he might like to be considered a star in circus circles,
to be the admiration of circus audiences, and to be regarded
with wondering awe by boys of his own age throughout the
country. But Kit was also a sensible boy. After all, this
preëminence was only of a physical character. A great acrobat or trapeze artist has no recognized place in society, and
his ambition is of a low character. While these reflections
were presenting themselves to his mind, Signor Oponto stood
by in silence, waiting for his answer. He thought that Kit's
hesitation was due to pecuniary considerations.

"What salary does Mr. Barlow pay you?" he asked, in a
businesslike tone.

"Twenty-five dollars a week."

"I will give you fifty, and engage you for a year."

He regarded Kit intently to see how this proposal struck him.

"You are very liberal, Signor Oponto," Kit began, but the manager interrupted him.

"I will also pay your board," he added; "and of course defray your expenses to Havana. Is that satisfactory?"

"It would be very much so but for one thing."

"What is that?"

"I doubt whether I shall remain in the business after this season."

"Why not? Don't you like it?"

"Yes, very well; but I prefer to follow some profession of a literary character. I am nearly prepared for college, and I may decide to continue my studies."

"But even your college students devote most of their time to baseball and rowing, I hear."

"Not quite so bad as that," answered Kit, with a smile.

"You don't refuse definitely, I hope."

"No; it may be that I may feel obliged to remain in the business. In that case I will give you the preference."

"That is all I can expect. Here is my card. Whenever you are ready, write me, and your communication will receive instant attention."

"Thank you, sir."

The next day Mlle. Lefroy resumed her work, the danger of meeting her husband having passed. She expressed her gratitude to Kit for serving as her substitute, and wished to make him a present of ten dollars, but he refused to accept it.

"I was glad of the chance to see what I could do on the trapeze," he said. "I never expect to follow it up, but I have already received an offer of an engagement in that line."

"So I heard. And you don't care to accept it?"

"No; I do not mean to be a circus performer permanently."

"You are right. It leads to nothing, and before middle life you are liable to find yourself unfitted for it."

CHAPTER XXXVI.

CLOSE OF THE CIRCUS.

DAYS and weeks flew swiftly by. September gave place to October, and the circus season neared its close. Already the performers were casting about for employment during the long, dull winter that must elapse before the next season.

"What are your plans, Kit?" asked Antonio Vincenti, who in private called his young associate by his real name.

"I don't know yet, Antonio. I may go to school."

"Have you saved money enough to keep you through the winter?"

"Yes; I have four hundred dollars in the wagon."

This is the expression made use of to indicate "in the hands of the treasurer."

"You've done better than my brother or I. We must work during the winter."

"Have you any chance yet?"

"Yes; we can go to work in a dime museum in Philadelphia for a month, and afterwards we will go to Chicago, where we were last winter. I could get a chance for you, too."

"Thank you, but I don't care to work in that way at present. If I went anywhere I would go to Havana, where I am offered a profitable engagement."

"Has Mr. Barlow said anything to you about next season?"

"Yes; but I shall make no engagement in advance. Something may happen which will keep me at home."

"Oh, you'll be coming round in the spring. You'll have the circus fever like all the rest of us."

Kit smiled and shook his head.

"I haven't been in the business long enough to get so much attached to it as you are," he said. "But at any rate, I shall come round to see my old friends."

The last circus performance was given in Albany, and the winter quarters were to be at a town twenty miles distant. Kit went through his acts with his usual success, and when he took off his circus costume, it was with a feeling that it might be the last time he would wear it.

The breaking up was not to take place till the next day, and he was preparing to spend the night in some Albany hotel.

He had taken off his tights, as has been said, and put on his street dress, when a tall man, with a frank, good-humored expression, stepped up to him.

"Are you Christopher Watson?" he asked.

"Yes," answered Kit, in surprise, for he had no recollection of having met the stranger before.

"Of course you don't know me, but I was a schoolfellow and intimate friend of your father."

"Then," said Kit, cordially, "I must take you by the hand. All my father's friends are my friends."

The face of the stranger lighted up.

"That's the way to talk," he said. "I see you are like your father. Shake hands again."

"But how did you know I was with Barlow's circus?" asked Kit, puzzled.

"Your uncle told me."

"Have you seen him lately?" asked Kit, quickly.

"No; I saw him about three months ago at Smyrna."

"What did he tell you about me?"

"He said you were a wayward lad, and preferred traveling with a circus to following an honest business."

"I am afraid you have got a wrong idea of me, then."

"Bless you, I knew your uncle before you were born. He is not at all like your father. One was as open as the day, the other was cunning, selfish, and foxy."

"I see you understand my uncle Stephen as well as I do."

"I ought to."

"Were you surprised to hear that I was traveling with a circus?"

"Well, I was; but your uncle told me one thing that surprised me more. He said that your father left nothing."

"That surprised me, too; but I have got some light on the subject and I feel in need of a friend and adviser."

"Then if you'll take Henry Miller for want of a better, I don't believe you'll regret it."

"I shall be glad to accept your kind offer, Mr. Miller. Now that you mention your name, I remember it very well. My father often spoke of you."

"Did he so?" said the stranger, evidently much gratified. "I am glad to hear it. Of all my school companions, your father was the one I liked best. And now, before we go any further, I want to tell you two things. First, I should have hunted you up sooner, but business called me to California, where I have considerable property. Next, having learned that you were left destitute, I decided to do something for the son of my old friend. So I took a hundred shares of stock in a new mine, which had just been put on the market when I reached 'Frisco, and I said to myself: 'That is for Kit Watson.' Well, it was a lucky investment. The shares cost me five dollars apiece, and just before I left California I sold them for fifty dollars apiece. What do you say to that?"

"Is it possible mining shares rise in value so fast?" asked Kit, in amazement.

"Well, sometimes they do, and sometimes they don't. Often it's the other way, and I don't advise you or anybody else that knows nothing about it to speculate in mining shares. It is a risky thing, and you are more apt to lose than to win. However, this turned out O. K., and you are worth five thousand dollars to-day, my boy."

"I don't know how to thank you, Mr. Miller," said Kit. "I can't seem to realize it."

"You needn't thank me at all. I did it for your father's sake, but now that I know you I am glad to do it for your own. When we get to New York I advise you to salt it down in government bonds, or in some other good reliable stock."

"I shall be glad to follow your advice, Mr. Miller."

"Then I'll invest all but five hundred dollars, for you may want to use that. What sort of a season have you had?"

"I've saved up four hundred dollars," said Kit, proudly.

"You don't say so! You must have got pretty good pay."

"Twenty-five dollars a week."

"Your uncle said you probably got two or three dollars a week."

"He probably thought so. He has no idea I have been so well paid. I chose to keep it from him."

"You said you wanted to ask my advice about something."

"Yes, sir."

"Why not come round to the Delavan and take a room? I am staying there, and I will tell the clerk to pick you out a room next to mine."

"I will do so. I intended to stay at some hotel to-night. This is the last night of the circus. To-morrow we close up and separate. I shall draw my money and bid good-by to my circus friends."

"I am glad of that. We will keep together. I have neither chick nor child, Kit, and if you'll accept me as your guardian I'll do the best I can for you. But perhaps you prefer to go back to your uncle."

Kit shook his head.

"I should never do that," he said, "especially after what I have learned during my trip."

"Let it keep till to-morrow, for we are both tired. Now get ready and we'll go to the Delavan."

Kit was assigned a nice room next to Mr. Miller, where he passed a comfortable night.

The next day he revealed to his new friend the discoveries he had made in his uncle's old home in Pennsylvania—his uncle's poverty up to the time of his brother's death, and the evident falseness of his claim to have lent him large sums of money, in payment of which he had coolly appropriated his entire estate.

His new friend listened to this story in amazement.

"I knew Stephen Watson to be unprincipled," he said, "but I didn't think him as bad as that. He has swindled you shamefully."

"Just my idea, Mr. Miller."

"While he has carefully feathered his own nest. This wrong must be righted."

"It was my intention to find some good lawyer, and ask his advice."

"We'll do it, Kit. But first of all, I'll go with you to this town in Pennsylvania, and obtain the necessary testimony sworn to before a justice. Then we'll find a good lawyer, and move on the enemy's works."

"I will be guided by your advice entirely, Mr. Miller."

"It will be a satisfaction to me to get even with your uncle. To swindle his own nephew in this barefaced manner! We'll bring him up with a short turn, Kit!"

The next day Kit and his new friend left Albany.

CHAPTER XXXVII.

KIT COMES HOME.

ONE morning James Schuyler, Kit's old acquaintance at Smyrna, received a letter from Kit, in which he said: "Our circus season is ended, but I am detained a few days by important business. I will tell you about it when we meet. If you see my uncle, tell him that I expect to reach Smyrna somewhere about the twenty-fifth of October."

"I wonder what Kit's important business can be," thought James. "I hope it is something of advantage to him."

James happened to meet Stephen Watson an hour later.

"Mr. Watson," he said, "I had a letter from Kit this morning."

"Indeed!"

"He says that his circus season is over."

"And he is out of employment," said Watson, his lip curling.

"I suppose so; he expects to reach Smyrna somewhere about the twenty-fifth of the month."

Stephen Watson smiled, but said nothing.

"No doubt he will find it very convenient to stay at home through the winter," he reflected. "Well, he must think I am a fool to take back a boy who has defied my authority."

It was Saturday, and Ralph was home from boarding school.

"Ralph," said his father, "I bring you good news."

"What is it, pa?"

"Your cousin will be home from the circus toward the last of next week."

"Who told you? Did he write you?"

"He wrote to James Schuyler, who told me."

"I suppose he expects you will give him a home through the winter."

"You may rest easy, Ralph. He won't have his own way with me, I can assure you."

"What shall you do, pa?"

"I shall see Bickford about taking him back. I have occasion to go over there on Monday to have the horse shod, and I can speak to him about it."

Ralph laughed.

"That will bring down his pride," he said. "I suppose he will beg off."

"He will find me firm as a rock. What I decide upon I generally carry through."

"Good for you, pa! I was afraid you would weaken."

"You don't know me, my son. I have been patient and bided my time. Your cousin presumed to set up his will against mine. He has got along thus far because he has made a living by traveling with a circus. Now the circus season is at an end, and he is glad enough to come back to me."

On Monday Stephen Watson rode over to Oakford, and made it in his way to call on Aaron Bickford.

"Have you got a boy, Mr. Bickford?" he asked.

"I had one, but he left me last Saturday. He didn't suit me."

This was the blacksmith's interpretation of it. The truth was the boy became disgusted with the treatment he received and the fare provided at his employer's table, and left him without ceremony.

"How would you like to take back my nephew?"

"Has he come back?" asked the blacksmith, pricking up his ears.

"Not yet; but I expect him back toward the end of next week."

"Has he left the circus?"

"The circus has left him. That is, it has closed for the season. He has sent word to a boy in Smyrna that he will be back in a few days."

"He gave me a great deal of trouble, Mr. Watson."

"Just so, and I thought you might like to get even with him," said Stephen Watson, looking significantly at the blacksmith.

"It would do me good to give him a flogging," said Aaron Bickford.

"I shan't interfere," replied Watson. "The boy has acted badly and he deserves punishment."

"Yes, I'll take him back," said the blacksmith. "I guess he'll stay this time," he added, grimly.

"I think he will have to. There won't be any circus to give him employment."

"He's a good strong boy, and he can make a good blacksmith, if he has a mind to."

"You must make him have a mind to," said Stephen Watson.

When the horse was shod he got into the carriage and drove away.

After this interview Mr. Bickford seemed in unusually good spirits, so much so that his wife inquired: " Have you had any good luck, Aaron? "

" What makes you ask? "

" Because you look unusually chipper. I was hopin' somebody had died and left you a fortune."

" Well, not exactly, wife; but I've heard something that makes me feel good."

" What's that? "

" Stephen Watson, of Smyrna, was over here this morning."

" Well? "

" He says that boy Kit is coming home in a few days."

" What if he is? "

" He's goin' to bring him over here, and apprentice him to me again."

" I should think once would be enough, considerin' how he treated you."

" He ain't goin' to serve me so again, you may bet on that. I'm goin' to have my way this time."

" Ain't you afraid he'll run away again? "

" Not much. The circus has shut up, and he'll have to stay with me, or starve. His uncle tells me I can punish him when I think he deserves it."

" I hope you won't be disappointed, Mr. Bickford, but that boy's rather hard to handle."

" I know it, but I'm the one that can handle him."

" You thought so before, the evening we went to the show."

" I know so this time."

CHAPTER XXXVIII.

CONCLUSION.

SEVERAL days passed. On Thursday afternoon Kit arrived in Smyrna, accompanied by his generous California friend, Henry Miller. They put up at the hotel, and after dinner Kit walked over to the house occupied by his uncle.

Mr. Watson saw him from the window, and hastening to the door, opened it himself.

" Good-afternoon, Uncle Stephen," said Kit.

" So you're back! " said his uncle, curtly.

" Yes; did you expect me? "

" James Schuyler told me you were coming."

" Yes, I wrote him that he might inform you."

" That was a good thought of yours. I have made arrangements for you."

" What arrangements? "

" I shall take you over to Oakford on Saturday, and place you with Aaron Bickford to learn the blacksmith's trade. This time I'd advise you not to run away."

Kit didn't exhibit any dismay when his uncle informed him of the plan he had arranged for him.

" I will talk this over with you, Uncle Stephen," he said. " With your permission I will go into the house."

" You can stay here till Saturday. Then you will go with me to Oakford."

Kit followed his uncle into the house. " I have something important to say to you, Uncle Stephen," he went on. " Sit down, and I will tell you what I have discovered within the last few months."

Stephen Watson anxiously awaited Kit's communication.

" Can he have found out? " he asked himself. " But no! it is impossible."

" I will give you five minutes to tell me your astonishing discovery," he said, with an attempt at his usual sneer.

" I may need a longer time, but I will be as quick as I can. Among the places where our circus exhibited was Glendale, Pennsylvania. Remembering that you once lived there, I made inquiries about you in the village. I saw the house where you lived for many years. Judge of my surprise when I learned that you were always in extreme poverty. Then I recalled your story of having lent my father ten thousand dollars, in payment of which you took the bulk of his property. I mentioned it, and found that it was pronounced preposterous. I discovered that, on the other hand, you were frequently the recipient of money gifts from my poor father. In return for this you have attempted to rob his son. The note which you presented against the estate was undoubtedly a forgery. But even had it been genuine, the property of which you took possession must have amounted to twenty thousand dollars at the very least."

Stephen Watson had not interrupted Kit by a word. He was panic-stricken, and absolutely did not know what to say. He finally succeeded in answering hoarsely: " This is an outrageous falsehood, Christopher Watson. It is an ingenious scheme to rob me of what rightfully belongs to me. You must be a fool to think I am going to be frightened by a boy's wild fiction. Leave my house! I would have allowed you to stay till Saturday, but this is too much. If you come here again, I will horsewhip you! "

But even when he was making his threat his face was pallid and his glance uneasy.

At this moment the bell rang.

Kit himself answered the call, and returned with his friend, Henry Miller.

"Why, it is Mr. Miller!" said Stephen Watson, who had not forgotten that Miller was very wealthy. "When did you return from California?"

"Kit, have you told your uncle?" asked Henry Miller, ignoring this greeting.

"Yes, and he orders me to leave the house."

"Hark you, Stephen Watson!" said Henry Miller, sternly. "You are in a bad box. For over a week Kit and I have been looking up matters, and we are prepared to prove that you have outrageously defrauded him out of his father's estate. We have enlisted a first-class lawyer in the case, and now we come to you to know whether you will surrender or fight."

"Mr. Miller, this is very strange. Are you in the plot too?"

"Don't talk of any plots, Stephen Watson. Your fraud is so transparent that I wonder you dared to hope it would succeed. You probably presumed upon Kit's being a boy of an unsuspicious nature. But he has found a friend, who was his father's friend before him, and who is determined that he shall be righted."

"I defy you!" exclaimed Stephen Watson, recklessly, for he saw that submission would be ruin and leave him penniless.

"Wait a minute! I'll give you another chance. Do you know what we are prepared to prove? Well, I will tell you. We can prove that you are not only a swindler but a forger, and our success will consign you to a prison cell. You deserve it, no doubt, but you shall have a chance."

"What terms do you offer?" asked Stephen Watson, overwhelmed by the conviction that what Miller said was true.

"Surrender unconditionally, restore to Kit his own property, and——"

"But it will leave me penniless!" groaned Stephen Watson.

"Just as I supposed. In Kit's behalf, I will promise that you shall not starve. You once kept a small grocery store, and understand the trade. We will set you up in that business wherever you choose, and will give you besides a small income, say three hundred dollars a year, so that you may be able to live modestly."

"But Ralph, my poor boy, what will become of him?"

"I will pay the expenses of his education," said Kit, "and when he leaves school, I will make him an allowance so that he can enter a store and qualify himself to earn his own living. He won't be able to live as he has lived, but he shall not suffer."

"It is more than either of you deserve," said Henry Miller. "I was not in favor of treating you so generously, but Kit, whom you have defrauded, insisted upon it. You ought to thank him on your knees."

Stephen Watson did not speak. He looked the picture of misery.

"Do you agree to this?" asked Mr. Miller.

"I must!" replied Watson, sullenly.

It made a great sensation in Smyrna when Kit took his proper place as the true master of his dead father's estate. Stephen Watson left town suddenly, and Ralph followed him. No sorrow was felt for his reverse of fortune, for he had made no friends in the town. He and Ralph settled down in a small Western city, and started a grocery store. From time to time Kit receives abject letters, pleading for more money, and sometimes he sends it, but always against the advice of Henry Miller, who says rightly that Stephen Watson already fares better than he deserves.

Ralph is turning out badly. His pride received a severe shock when his cousin was raised above him, and he has formed bad habits which in time will wreck him physically, unless he turns over a new leaf.

It is hardly necessary to say that Kit decided not to learn the blacksmith's trade. His old employer, Aaron Bickford, has tried hard to get into his good graces and secure his trade, but Kit employs another man for whom he has a greater respect.

Kit has made more than one visit to the worthy Mayor Grant from whom he received so much kindness when a young acrobat, and a marked partiality for Evelyn, the mayor's pretty daughter, may some day lead to a nearer connection between the families.

Good, like bad fortune, seldom comes singly, and besides recovering his own property, Kit finds himself the favorite and presumed heir of Henry Miller, the wealthy Californian, who has taken up his home with our hero. Last summer they took a trip to California, and Kit was charmed with the wonderful Yosemite Valley and the Geysers. He has decided to become a lawyer, though he will be in a position to live without employment of any kind.

A few months after his return, Kit read in the paper of the killing of Dick Hayden, the miner, in a drunken brawl at Coalville.

He at once took steps to seek out the daughter, Janet, who had rendered him such signal service when he was captured by the ruffians, and brought her to Smyrna, where he provided a happy home for her in a family of his acquaintance.

Nor has Kit forgotten his circus friends. Last year, when Barlow's circus returned from its wanderings, he invited those whom he knew best, the giant, and his two brother acrobats, and Mlle. Lefroy, to pass a week as his guests. For the sake of old times and experiences he is always ready to help professionals, and has been a friend in need to many. He knows that with all their weaknesses they are generous to a fault, and ready to divide their last dollar with a needy comrade. There are some who think Kit shows a strange taste in keeping up acquaintance with his old associates, but like his friend, Charlie Davis, who has also retired from the circus, he will always have a kindly feeling for those with whom he traveled when a Young Acrobat.

ONE TRUE HEART

By Frances Henshaw Baden

A PLEASANT, gentle-looking girl was seated under the shade
of a great oak tree. There was a wistful look in her brown
eyes, as she followed the form of a handsome, dashing-look-
ing fellow going down the path, with a brilliant little beauty
hanging on his arm.

"Oh, I wish it was time to go! I just hate picnics," she
was saying to herself, when lounging, careless and free,
came Tom Howard, and said:

"Everybody has paired off but you and me, Miss Grayson.
Oh, I'm not going to call you so. My sisters call you Annie,
and I think I might. You are tired, I see, and the day not
half spent. Come! I'm going to try and make myself agreeable, and perhaps the hours may be endured until the going-
home time comes. Now, Annie, I know what you were
thinking about when I came up."

Annie shook her head, and said:

"Indeed you do not."

"Very well, if I'm right, you will own up?"

A smiling assent from Annie.

"You were hating picnics, because a certain handsome fellow is devoting himself to a would-be belle!"

Annie blushed so deeply that Tom said:

"That's all right. I have a knack of reading looks. I'm
glad you are not an acknowledged beauty, Annie. I detest
having to talk to such girls. One has got to keep, while
with them, the same look of admiration on his face, and

neither see nor hear anybody else. It is really good to have a sensible girl to talk to."

"Indeed, I'd just like to be as pretty as Miss Oakley! Just see how Harry keeps beside her." Annie's lips quivered just a little then. Ah, she had let her secret slip out!

Tom felt as if he would enjoy giving Harry Cleveland a good thrashing. He felt sure he had been trifling with the gentle girl's heart. But Tom thought changing the conversation would help matters just then.

"Have you ever spent a winter in town, Annie?"

Annie never had; but said:

"I would like to, ever so much."

"Katie has mother's commands to either bring you, or the promise of your coming before Christmas," Tom said. "And, then, I'll promise you the gayest time you ever had."

On and on Tom talked, telling of the "time" they had last season, and relating anecdotes and jokes, so that, notwithstanding an occasional sigh, when Harry came in sight, Annie was surprised when some one called:

"The boat is coming!"

Tom managed to catch Harry alone on the way home, and say:

"Cleveland, since I've been visiting down here I've heard your name connected with Miss Grayson's. Now, I want to know if I will be trespassing on somebody else's ground?"

"No, indeed; not *mine*. Annie is the dearest little *friend* in the world. That's all. Possibly in time there is no knowing but I might have been *rash* enough to—well—ah!—excuse me, there is Miss Oakley, beautiful and rich. Good evening. You have my best wishes."

"The consummate puppy. He is not worthy of her. Never mind. My name's not Tom Howard if I don't change his tune in less than six months."

Annie Grayson and Tom Howard's sister were schoolmates.

A sweet, simple, country girl was Annie, never having been farther than the little town of P——, where the seminary was.

Harry Cleveland had been visiting an uncle in the neighborhood for a few weeks, during which time he had amused himself with the gentle little Annie.

And she, poor girl, thought her heart must break when Harry left her to follow in the train with Miss Oakley's admirers.

Annie's father was only a "well-to-do farmer." And it cost him a considerable effort to give his daughter a suitable fit-out for a winter in town; but Annie had grown so sad he was glad to let her go. Annie had not entirely cast Harry from her heart. Some little hope of seeing him and winning him back lingered still when she arrived in B——.

What Tom had been doing I cannot just tell, but somehow, to Annie's immense surprise, the evening of her arrival she found herself surrounded by a half dozen very pleasant young gentlemen, each one seeming to vie with the other in attentions to her. Engagements for the opera, concert and lectures were made for her. In a few words, in less than a week after she reached B——, Annie Grayson was an acknowledged belle. No one called her a beauty. But one raved over her "bronze eyes;" another, her charming *naiveté;* a third, her sylph-like form. An artist friend of Tom's wanted to paint her picture. He, of course, knew true beauty. That was enough. It was the fashion to have De Vere paint one's portrait; and so, in a few weeks, Annie Grayson's picture was on exhibition in De Vere's studio. One would hardly have credited the change those weeks had wrought in the simple country girl, and for the better, too. She was not spoiled at all—only pleased and happy. She grew very easy and graceful in her manner. Her eyes were brighter, and laughing. She had gotten entirely over the wound made by Harry Cleveland, and was heart-whole and free for a while. Frequently she met Miss Oakley with Harry, but no longer she sighed for her beauty. Once or twice he had called, but finding Annie always with pleasant company, troubled himself no further. What it was that first drew so many admirers around Annie, Tom knew best; but no one wondered that she endeared herself to all who knew her.

Whispers were afloat that Miss Oakley's riches were in the oil regions, and after a while that no oil was there, consequently no riches for her. What it was I can't say; but Miss Oakley went home to P——, and Harry did not follow. About this time Harry's aunt came to town, bringing to Annie many little remembrances from home.

Of course Harry came with her—and somehow managed to get in the way of dropping in occasionally, much to the disgust of some of Annie's more persevering suitors. Harry never could bear opposition. First, because he wanted to run others off; and, again, because Miss Grayson was "the fashion" then. Harry began again his lovemaking. Wooing the little rustic and wooing the calm, assured city belle were two different things.

Annie laughed at him, not believing, or feigning not to believe, a word he said. At length—in perfect desperation, Harry sought Tom, and begged his help.

"Cleveland, months ago I came to you. I would not have tried to win her from you. You told me to go ahead, I had your best wishes. I cannot understand this change—— "

"Nor I, Tom. I only know I *love* her *now*—I do, upon my honor," said Harry.

"Has not the little piece of fun, the report of an uncle in India, whose heiress she is to be, had this powerful effect?" Tom asked, a contemptuous smile curling his lips.

"No, no. Of course I know better than that. You remember my aunt's intimate connection with her family. No, Tom, I *love* her—I'd marry her to-day, and work for her cheerfully all the days of my life."

"And Miss Oakley——"

"She—ah, well! I only *imagined* I was in love with her," Harry said, looking considerably embarrassed.

"Well, Cleveland, *I* am not one of Miss Grayson's suitors. If you can win her I shall not oppose you."

One after another of Annie's lovers had to content themselves with her friendship. Harry grew very hopeful, and Tom began to think his little game might not end just as he wished. He could resign her to anyone sooner than to Harry Cleveland. There was one young fellow to whom Tom had confessed his joke concerning the India wealth. When he knew Annie was poorer than himself, he wooed her more earnestly. In every way he was worthy of Annie.

Possibly, for a chance to learn the true state of her heart, Tom went to plead another's cause.

"Annie, may I speak a word for Noble? Can you not learn to love him? Poor fellow! he quite worships you," Tom said, "and I wish——"

"I wish I was home again," Annie said; and, dropping her head, she sobbed like a grieved child.

"Why, Annie, how can you talk so? What has worried you? Everybody loves you. You ought to be the happiest girl in the world," Tom said, trying to soothe her.

"I don't want everybody to love me, and everybody don't love me," sobbed Annie.

"Oh, you unreasonable little girl! Six months ago I found your heart almost breaking for the love of just one. You wanted to be beautiful for his sake. And now that all you wished for is yours, you are not happy. What more can you wish?"

"I wish I'd never come to town! I wish I just *knew* I

possessed the love of *one* true heart. What do I want with many?"

"Annie, I truly believe Harry loves you, if it is about him you are troubled. But I would sooner give you to Noble—— "

She turned, with her eyes flashing. What she would have said was interrupted by Harry's entrance. Tom left the room. A half hour after, with a heavy step, the young man came forth, and joining Tom on the porch, said:

"It is all over with me, Howard. I would give years of my life to recall the last six months. *Then* I might have won her, and now she is lost to me forever!"

"Whom does she care for, I'd like to know?" Tom asked.

Harry shook his head sadly, and passed out a wiser man. Later that afternoon Tom found out.

"I wish I had tried to win her myself," he said. "I shall never love another so well. I wonder if her heart is free? I've a mind to try."

Annie, Tom's sister, and a little brother sat out on the porch watching the sunset, when the loud report of a gun was heard in the house. The little boy rushed in, and a moment after came flying back, crying:

"Oh, Tom is shot! Tom is killed!"

All ran in—all but Annie. Without a word she had fallen to the ground. Ten minutes after, when they found her, she was still to all appearance lifeless.

It was so long before she opened her eyes that they had grown terribly anxious.

With a wild look at last she turned from one to the other. Then her gaze rested on one nearest to her. With a glad cry she put forth her arms.

Tom knew *all*, then, and kneeling beside her said, in a whisper low:

"My darling, my own, be *sure* of the love of one true heart. Are you satisfied with mine, love?"

"Are you hurt?" she asked, the warm blood returning to the pale face.

"Not the least, only upset by the shock. I would not have minded a considerable hurt for such a cure," Tom said.

And then, when they were alone, he asked again:

"Are you happy now, Annie?"

"Who would not be," she answered, "when sure of the love of one true heart?"

THE END

Printed in the United States
3997

9 781589 637542